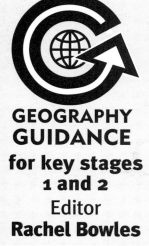

GEOGRAPHY
GUIDANCE
for key stages
1 and 2
Editor
Rachel Bowles

Studying Contrasting UK Localities

PENNY SWEASEY

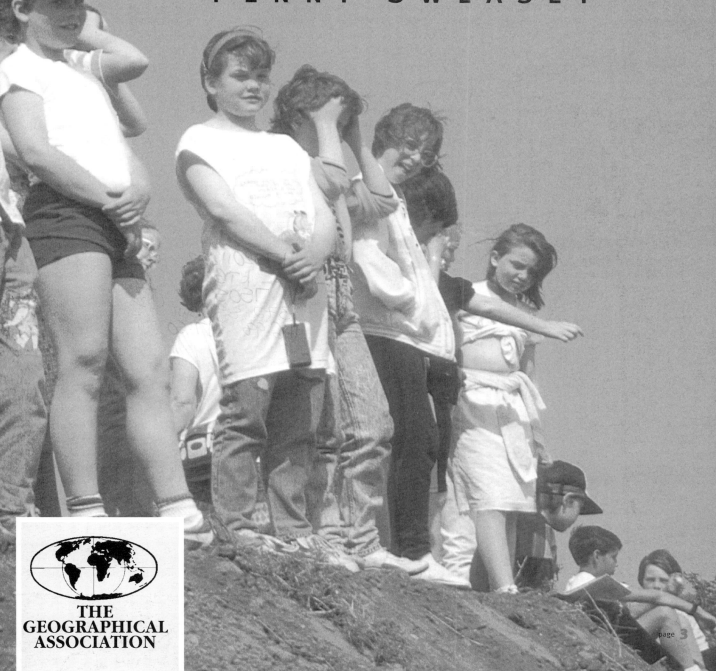

THE
**GEOGRAPHICAL
ASSOCIATION**

Acknowledgements

The author and publishers are grateful to the following:
Teachers in Stockport, Tameside and Trafford who trialled this material as part of a 10 day course at The Manchester Metropolitan University in 1996.

Gaynor Grabner, Janice Adams and the children in their classes for providing material for worksheets and photographs.

Extract from *Expectations in Geography at Key Stages 1 and 2* on pages 46-47 reproduced with kind permission of SCAA.

Map extracts on pages 24, 29 and 37 reproduced with kind permission of Experian Goad Ltd, Hatfield, Hertfordshire.

Cover photo: Mo Morron
Frontispiece: Chris Garnett

ISBN 1 899085 44 0
First published 1997

Impression number 10 9 8 7 6 5 4 3 2 1
Year 2000 1999 1998 1997

Published by the Geographical Association, Solly Street, Sheffield S1 4BF. The Geographical Association is a registered charity: no 313129.

The Publications Officer of the GA would be happy to hear from other potential authors who have ideas for geography books. You may contact the Officer via the GA at the address above. The views expressed in this publication are those of the author and do not necessarily represent those of the Geographical Association.

Edited by Hazel Wright, Hart McLeod and Rose Pipes
Design and typesetting: Ledgard Jepson Ltd
Printed and bound in England by Stephen Austin, Hertford

Studying Contrasting UK Localities

Editor's preface

The *Geography guidance* series is designed to be a source of quick reference and practical help to teachers. It is the Geographical Association's 'fast response' to teachers' needs and to perceived gaps in the published literature, and such needs will be answered briefly but comprehensively. The series has two strands, primary and secondary.

Primary Guidance is intended to help primary teachers plan for and implement the geography Programme of Study (PoS) for key stages 1 and 2. It is aimed at non-specialist primary teachers, particularly those responsible for geography coordination.

Each book in the series will deal with a particular aspect of teaching primary geography, but some elements will be common to all:

- emphasis on the enquiry process
- suggested strategies and associated activities
- exploration of IT opportunities
- coverage of progression, differentiation and assessment
- freely photocopiable exemplars and blank planning sheets
- guidance on the nature and use of resources
- suggestions for the development of INSET work.

I hope that you will find the guidance helpful; please let me know if you have any suggestions for subjects which we should address in the series.

Rachel Bowles
June 1997

Contents

Introduction

This book will help teachers at key stages 1 and 2 to plan for and implement the study of contrasting UK localities.

It is aimed particularly at non-specialist geographers (those who 'dropped' geography at 14 and also may have received little or no INSET since), but geography specialists also should find that it can support them in developing good practice in their school.

The book gives:

- a framework of planning steps
- a sample of suggested activities for studying geography and other subjects in the locality, including worked examples
- photocopiable planning sheets
- guidance on choosing resources
- suggestions for INSET activities to introduce the ideas to your colleagues

It is expected that children will have been introduced to the skills and techniques of observation, recording and analysis in their local area and that their knowledge of the home locality will form a foundation upon which comparisons with different places can be built.

Photo: Joan Crookes

1: Why study a contrasting UK locality?

The statutory requirements provide children, for the first time, with an entitlement to study somewhere other than their local area, thus presenting them with the opportunity to gain better, richer understanding of real places and the people who live in them. Small children have a natural interest in people and places and the National Curriculum requires teachers to develop this curiosity. Some educational reasons for studying other localities are given in Figure 1.

Studying other places provides opportunities for children to:
1. use and develop their interest and natural curiosity about places
2. explore ideas and skills and extend their language
3. develop their existing knowledge and understanding of other places
4. examine and clarify their existing experience and awareness of places
5. develop spatial awareness towards a global scale
6. recognise their interdependence with the rest of the world
7. build positive attitudes towards other people
8. build up a global perspective from their local perspective
9. value diversity in places, environments and cultures
10. combat ignorance and bias to avoid stereotyping and prejudice.

(Adapted from Catling, S. (1995) 'Wider Horizons: the children's charter', *Primary Geographer*, issue 20)

Figure 1: Ten good reasons for studying other places

2: What are the statutory requirements?

Geographical investigation and enquiry are essential elements of National Curriculum geography at key stages 1 and 2. In both key stages children are required to study the local area and a contrasting locality. At key stage 1 the chosen contrasting locality should be an area of similar size to the school locality, that is, the school buildings and grounds and their immediate vicinity - the surrounding area within easy access. This small, manageable area, the size of a village or part of a town or city, can be either in the United Kingdom or overseas.

At key stage 2 the two contrasting localities to be studied should include one locality in the United Kingdom and one chosen from Asia and the Southern continents. The localities should be larger than at key stage 1, equivalent to the school catchment area. The four geographical themes at key stage 2 may be studied 'as part of the studies of places' thereby extending opportunities for studying other localities. Together the study of both places and themes requires you to plan for work at a range of scales and in a range of contexts, including the United Kingdom, the European Union and the wider world.

This book covers work on a contrasting locality in the United Kingdom. A companion book, *Studying Distant Places* by Maureen Weldon, considers contrasting localities in the wider world. Both emphasise that children should be given opportunities to undertake fieldwork activities (observe, question and record), to develop geographical skills and find out about geographical themes in a variety of contexts.

3: How do I choose a locality?

At key stage 1 the children should study a locality where the physical or human features (or both) contrast with those of the immediate vicinity of the school. At key stage 2 the locality covers a larger area which has to be set in context with other places. Localities can be urban or rural but whichever type you choose there should be plenty of opportunities for investigation. Select an area where the land use is mixed, where it is safe to walk around (for example, a pedestrian precinct, an enclosed heritage site) and where children will be able to see some patterns emerge.

Preparing and planning a locality study, whether at home or away, requires a great deal of time and effort. It is a good idea to visit the area in advance. The opportunities for fieldwork, enquiry and map work can be more easily recognised in the field than from talking to others, looking at maps or reading study packs. A visit facilitates the solution of logistical

problems of time and distance. You may decide to arrange a residential visit using a field centre equipped with resource material and expert advice.

The ideas in this book are mainly settlement studies but they could be adapted for a variety of different places for fieldwork at shopping centres, industrial sites, farms and (at key stage 1) in school grounds both at home and away. Some of the activities are more complex and are suitable for junior classes, but all can be adapted for younger groups.

Figure 2 will guide you through the process of selecting the best place for a contrasting UK locality study. There are a number of possible starting points and pathways and the questions are intended to help you assess your specific needs. You will need to consider additional questions related to your school and the children you teach.

Photo: Penny Sweasey

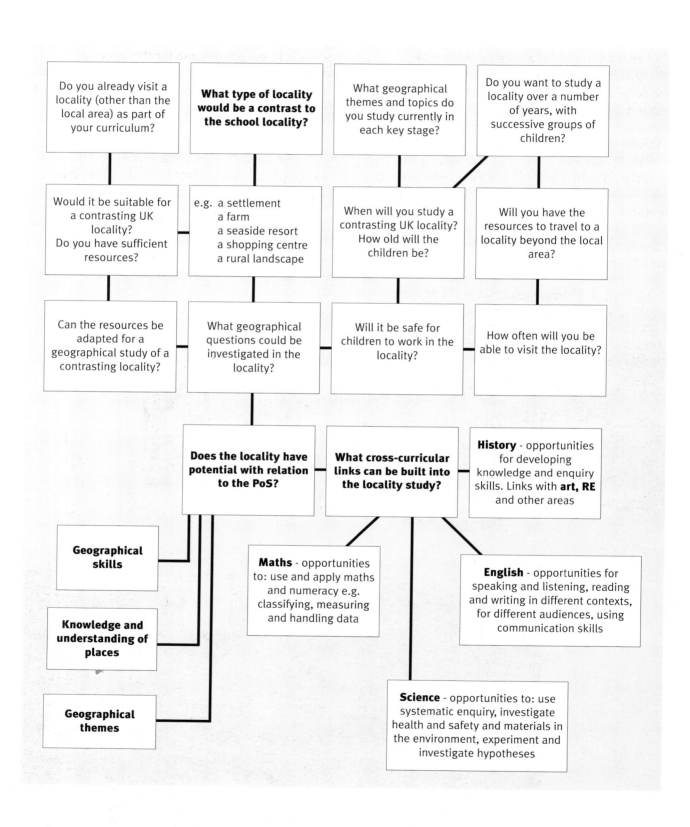

Do you already visit a locality (other than the local area) as part of your curriculum?

What type of locality would be a contrast to the school locality?

What geographical themes and topics do you study currently in each key stage?

Do you want to study a locality over a number of years, with successive groups of children?

Would it be suitable for a contrasting UK locality?
Do you have sufficient resources?

e.g. a settlement
a farm
a seaside resort
a shopping centre
a rural landscape

When will you study a contrasting UK locality? How old will the children be?

Will you have the resources to travel to a locality beyond the local area?

Can the resources be adapted for a geographical study of a contrasting locality?

What geographical questions could be investigated in the locality?

Will it be safe for children to work in the locality?

How often will you be able to visit the locality?

Does the locality have potential with relation to the PoS?

What cross-curricular links can be built into the locality study?

History - opportunities for developing knowledge and enquiry skills. Links with **art, RE** and other areas

Geographical skills

Maths - opportunities to: use and apply maths and numeracy e.g. classifying, measuring and handling data

English - opportunities for speaking and listening, reading and writing in different contexts, for different audiences, using communication skills

Knowledge and understanding of places

Geographical themes

Science - opportunities to: use systematic enquiry, investigate health and safety and materials in the environment, experiment and investigate hypotheses

Figure 2: Pathways for choosing a locality: some questions to consider

4: UK locality studies in the curriculum

The characteristics of a locality selected for study at key stage 1 will be very different from those of an area studied for key stage 2. At key stage 1 it is likely that the school vicinity will comprise a residential estate or rural village. The extended catchment area at key stage 2, however, may well include a High Street and associated urban activities or (in a rural context) may include a variety of clearly visible physical features. Because of these differences it is useful to study the implications of the PoS for both stages and for different environments in detail (see below). The findings could be applied equally to both the home locality and the contrasting locality: the chief distinction lies in the greater opportunity for collecting data over a longer period of time in the local area.

The Programmes of Study for geography comprise four strands: How to learn; Geographical skills; Places and localities and Geographical themes. These are good starting points for your planning - all four areas should feature in a locality study. The panels on pages 12 to 14 identify those parts of the PoS which relate to locality studies in the UK.

Photo: Penny Sweasey

Photo: Paula Richardson

1 How to learn about geography

From the time they are born, children are developing their own personal geography; exploring and observing and finding out about their surroundings. Through a practical play-based curriculum Nursery and Early Years provision continues to develop children's natural curiosity whilst giving them the opportunity to ask questions, to investigate their ideas and make sense of their surroundings. The geographical opportunities that you can build into your curriculum are listed in paragraph 1 of the PoS at both key stages.

- **Investigate the human and physical features of their surroundings KS1 1a**

  Features are distinctive parts or elements which make up a landscape. These include physical features such as mountains, slopes, rivers and vegetation, and human or built features such as buildings, roads, pylons, railways, farms.

  Landmarks are prominent features in the environment that children and adults recognise, such as churches, rivers and bridges, playgrounds, high hills, supermarkets, radio masts.

- **Investigate places and themes across a widening range of scales KS2 1a**

  Areas: start at school and move into local, regional, national, European and global contexts.

  Themes: start at a single house then study street, estate, village, town, city and metropolis; or look at a stream, then a small local river, major river and continental river.

- **Ask geographical questions based on direct experience and fieldwork KS1 & 2 1b**

  Where is this place? Why is it here? What is it like? Why is it like this? How is it changing?

- **Recognise and explain geographical patterns KS2 1c**

  Why are the shops in the town centre? Why are the houses built in the valley? Why do sheep graze on the high land? Where is the weather best? What routes do the buses follow?

- **Become aware of how places fit into a broader geographical context KS2 1d**

  Children's addresses: house number, road, neighbourhood, town, county, country, continent. Recognising that their neighbourhood is part of a large town, that the UK is part of Europe, that buses link several towns together, that motorways carry goods from one part of the country to another.

2 Geographical skills

Children can learn a wide range of geographical skills and techniques based on fieldwork and classwork, using primary and secondary sources of data, such as maps, globes, measuring equipment, photographs and IT. These skills and techniques are listed in paragraphs 2 and 3 of the Programmes of Study at each key stage. At key stage 1 geographical skills are an integral part of the learning environment. The requirements at key stage 2 are more specific. The following exemplars come from a pedestrian study which could initially have begun as a data gathering exercise for maths. They illustrate the variety of geographical possibilities.

- **Observe and ask questions about geographical features and issues KS2 2a**

  Which is the busiest pavement in the town centre? Is there a need for a new pelican crossing?

- **Record evidence KS2 2b**

  Design a tally chart to count pedestrians on different pavements around the town centre.

- **Use field work techniques KS2 3b**

  Work out the best way to count people.

- **Use IT KS2 3f**

  Take photographs of the busy locations, enter the data on a spreadsheet.

- **Analyse evidence, draw conclusions and communicate findings KS2 2c**

  Collect and compare graphs from tally charts to find the busiest pedestrian route.

- **Make maps and plans at different scales KS2 3c**

  Draw bar graphs on to a base map; make a sketch map to show other possible survey areas.

- **Use geographical vocabulary KS2 3a**

  Describe the findings using locational terms; suggest a location e.g. by a pelican crossing.

- **Use and interpret maps at different scales KS2 3d**

  Find the answer to the question 'Why are some places busier than others?' using street and OS maps.

- **Use secondary sources of evidence KS2 3e**

  Find out which department is responsible for road safety and obtain official information.

- **Use Information Technology KS2 3f**

  Write to the appropriate local authority department (probably planning) with the findings of the school survey.

3 Places and localities

Places give children a context in which to develop their geographical skills. Place knowledge ranges from studying the immediate vicinity to setting their own location in a world context. Children should develop location knowledge based on the maps in the PoS.

The chosen UK locality must be one in which:
the physical and/or human features contrast with those in the locality of the school, and of a similar size to the school locality studied (i.e. the school grounds and immediate vicinity at key stage 1, the school catchment area at key stage 2). **Para 4**

The focus for locality studies should be:

- **The main physical and human features that give the localities their character KS1 & 2 5a**

  Natural features such as hills, rivers, woodland, steep and gentle slopes.

  Built features such as roads, houses, churches, shops, schools, reservoirs, quarries, industrial concerns.

- **Environmental issues KS2 5a**

  Issues which affect the character of the above features such as water and air pollution from industry and traffic.

  Proposals for changes to markets, shopping precincts, open space.

- **How the school and the contrasting locality are similar and different KS1 & 2 5b**

  The age of the buildings. What the buildings are used for. The jobs that people do in each place. How land is used. Whether it is a built up area or in the countryside. If the countryside is hilly or flat. The number of trees (if any) seen from the classroom window.

- **How weather affects people and their surroundings KS1 5c**

  Places for shelter from cold, heat, wind and rain. The activities that take place in the locality. How weather has affected building materials.

- **How land and buildings are used KS1 5d**

  Is the land built upon or are there open spaces? When were buildings built? Has the land always been used in the same way as now? What are different buildings used for? Is the land used for growing things, or for leisure activities?

- **How the features of the localities influence the nature and location of human activities KS2 5c**

  How the industrial sites are near the bypass or near the river. How the bigger houses are near open space. How the buildings get taller towards the town centre.

- **About recent or proposed changes in the localities KS2 5d**

  The effect of shops closing on the local parade. The use of a redundant school, factory or church site. The effect of traffic calming measures (barriers and humps) or pedestrianisation of a shopping area.

- **How the localities are set within a broader geographical context and linked to other places KS2 5e**

  How some of the above features are characteristic of the larger area in which they are set such as a town, major valley, major upland area. How the people and products of industry supply or are linked with other parts of the UK, Europe and the world.

4 Geographical themes

Additionally, locality studies can be a context for studying geographical themes. These are the broad subject areas which should be studied at a range of scales from local to national **KS2 6**. At a local scale they form part of the UK locality study.

The quality of the environment:

- **Attractive and unattractive features KS1 6a**

  Children to express likes and dislikes about buildings, views, tidiness or pollution, different parts of the school buildings and playground.

- **How the environment is changing KS1 6b**

  Changes to the local park, demolished housing, a new road crossing, a new supermarket.

- **How the quality of the environment can be sustained and improved KS1 6c**

  Ways of looking after the environment - with children as active participants in environmental care, local issues and projects which affect their lives - playgrounds, cycle lanes.

Rivers:
- **Rivers and their effect on the landscape Para 7**

  Look at valleys and slopes caused by rivers, how people use rivers for leisure, work and transport, and how these activities affect the locality. The contrasting area could well provide scope for appreciating parts of 7a and 7b which are not possible in the home locality.

Weather:
- **How weather varies between places and over time Para 8**

  Microclimate study can look at variations in site conditions such as windy or sheltered corners of the playground. This provides insight into variations in the wider vicinity and other localities. A locality can be visited during different seasons to see if the weather has an effect on how the place looks and the activities taking place in it.

Settlement:
- **How settlements differ and change Para 9**

  Relate to the age, type and number of buildings, houses, layout of street, types of shops and services, building materials, connections to other places, history and future plans.

Environmental change:
- **How environments change Para 10**

  Does the locality look as if people care for the environment or has it been neglected?

  What are the signs of care and neglect?

  Is the environment being changed by new buildings? Is the change good or bad?

A number of locality studies with different geographical foci can be built into the curriculum plans for years 1 to 6. Figure 3 shows an example of a planning grid for key stages 1 and 2 in relation to the Locality of the school/Contrasting UK locality strand only. It demonstrates how a school might identify opportunities for studying UK localities, both in the local area and further afield. A similar grid to show where distant places fit into the curriculum plan is to be found in the companion book *Studying Distant Places* by Maureen Weldon. Similar plans could be drawn up for in-depth consideration of themes.

PoS/Year	1	2	3	4	5	6
Places studied	School buildings and grounds	The locality of the school. A contrasting locality.	The locality of the school and its vicinity.	The local area.	Contrasting locality (UK or overseas)	Contrasting locality (UK or overseas)
Places visited and sources	School/5 mins walk (class homes). Pictures and people	School vicinity; Farm visit; seaside visit; People, stories, videos.	Contrasts in the vicinity; street; supermarket; park; stream, pictures, maps,	Contrasting localities in the school area: shopping mall; country park; planned estate	Day visit to village or town centre; LEA field centre; make a video to exchange.	Residential visit e.g. Eyam, Flatford. Visual and written diary
Themes addressed	Likes/dislikes 6a. Changes 6b.	How the environment can be sustained and improved 6a,b,c.	Settlement 9b. Weather 8b. Rivers 7b. Environment 10a.	Settlement 9a,b. Weather 8a. Environmental change 10b.	Themes according to locality. Settlement 9c. Weather 8a,c.	Themes for locality. Rivers 7a,b. Settlement.
			Local scale increasing to national scale ——————————————————————————————➤			
Main opportunities	1a,b,c. 2. Direct observation,	1a,b,c. Observe, question, record, communicate,	1a,b,c,d. 2. Observe with increasing understanding and awareness ————————————➤ enquire, collect, record,	analyse and communicate...	... increasingly complex...	issues and relationships.
Main skills developed	All of paragraph 3 in varying combinations ◄——— All of paragraph 3 in varying combinations and increasing sophistication ———➤					
	Use geographical skills relevant to activity and location increasing range and complexity with experience and opportunity including IT					
Progression	Use of speaking and drawing to record familiar places.	Increased use of different forms of recording and communicating. Unfamiliar places.	Local scale and an increasing range of scales to National Scale. ——————————➤			
			Increasing ability to recognise and understand patterns. ——————————————➤			
			Increasing knowledge and understanding of places. ——————————————————➤			
			Ever widening context. ————————————————————————————————➤			
			Begin to supply geographical reasons and geographical explanations. ————➤			
Some activities	Built environment. A sense of place.	Urban trails. Land use mapping.	Urban trails; Sense of place; Physical and built environment.	Environmental quality; Safety survey; Data collecting surveys...	Sense of place; Land use mapping; Built environment	Safety survey; Observation trail; Extended project

Figure 3: An example of UK locality study coverage in key stages 1 and 2. (The numbers refer to the paragraphs and statements in the PoS)

5: What is good geography teaching?

Good geography teaching is concerned with encouraging children to develop a sense of place and to develop an enquiring attitude towards places which looks for spatial and temporal patterns and connections: in short to *think* like a geographer.

It is good geography practice to provide children with opportunities to investigate a number of different places as they grow older and more skilled. Children carrying out a detailed locality study in Year 5 or 6 should be building on skills learnt when working on previous smaller studies in the local area. A single locality study, however much knowledge and skill it develops, is not sufficient to address all aspects of the Programmes of Study, nor to achieve a rounded understanding of the nature of geography. Children need to develop a broader geographical awareness to provide a context within which to locate their own homes and other places. They should be familiar with maps, globes and atlases so they can find the places they hear about from relatives, on TV, and at school - including the localities they and other classes visit or research. Linking these places to their own surroundings is the beginning of developing a 'sense of place'.

How do I develop a sense of place?

Children are born naturally curious. This curiosity can be used to help them develop a sense of place and an enquiry approach to geography. Encourage children to ask geographical questions of and about real people and real places both in the classroom and when visiting different localities. Pitch the questions appropriately, focusing on small areas at a scale to which children can relate.

1 By asking geographical questions about a UK locality

A general view of a place (either local or distant) can stimulate a wealth of questions starting with 'Where is it?' Children can be encouraged to look for clues in the picture and inevitably discussion will stimulate further enquiry questions. The top photo opposite prompts general questions which could apply to many different localities.

The next set of questions is specific to the photograph. As children become more familiar with asking geographical questions, encourage them to pose their own questions about the detail on their photograph, perhaps for their friends to answer (e.g. what can you see to the right of the photo?).

Ask colleagues to try this out as an INSET activity - show them an example and then ask them to write their own questions around a photograph which has been mounted on a larger sheet of paper. Further examples of ways of working with photographs are given on page 26.

2 By talking and writing about places

Both visual and verbal images can build up a sense of the character of a place. Visiting places is vital and children will learn more if encouraged to observe closely and discuss their findings. Many great writers describe places in graphic detail. They instinctively recognise the balance between detail and general surroundings and how each contributes to the reader's sense of place.

How do I develop geographical thinking?

The panel on page 18 suggests ways of developing geographical - and literary - thinking. Each activity demands close observation and recording and communicating the results. Such communication contributes to the literacy programme as well as involving graphic activities. The exercises help children develop a balanced approach to looking at places. Question what initially seems strange, consider other elements in the surroundings and see if together they reveal the natural pressures and cultural influences upon a place. A good way of learning to avoid hasty, stereotypical judgements of any place is to consider how the home locality would appear to a visitor. What would you show your visitor? Remember there is no way you can stop your visitor seeing other

Where is it?

What is it?

What is it like?

Is it similar to the local area?

What is it used for?

What do people do here?

Is it changing?

Do you like this place?

Where is it near to?

What do other people think about this place?

Photo: Paula Richardson

How is it changing?

How did it get like this?

Do you think anyone lives here?

What can you see in the background?

Do you know what this place was built for?

What do you think this place is used for now?

Do you think the environment is looked after?

How has this changed since it was built?

What is this feature called?

Photo: Penny Sweasey

Do you like this place?

things - the Good, the Bad, and the Ugly! How would you describe your locality to your visitor? How would you describe your contrasting locality?

Some ideas to develop geographical thinking

- Collect examples of **The Good, the Bad and the Ugly** e.g. shop fronts, redevelopments, buildings or other features.

- **Well, I've Never Seen That Before!** Walk around a familiar place and try to spot some features that you have never looked at before.

- **Just One Photograph**. If you had to take a single photo to show what a place is like ... what view would you choose?

- **Make a Video**. Sometimes looking through a lens gives the viewer a different perspective on a place. Deciding what to include in a video can help to prioritise images and ideas.

- **My Favourite Place**. Use writing, drawing and collage to sum up feelings about a favourite or familiar place and then use this work as a comparison with another place.

- **For and Against**. Set up role-play activities and scenarios to debate planning issues; try to get people who are actively involved to visit the school.

- **Planning a Site**. Find a space which can be developed, or a location which might become a green site, and ask children to make a plan for the area. Hold a competition for the best design. This activity might follow on from planning spaces in the playground.

- A variation on this idea is **Fill in the Gap**. Either on paper or in discussion using photographs and observations encourage children to make decisions about how they would fill in a space between two other buildings.

- Children can **Make a Model Street**. Often it is easier to talk and write about maps and plans when you have a 3-D model. This is a good way of linking practical classroom activities with fieldwork.

- A **Tourist Information** poster or leaflet can be designed to summarise the attractions of a place. Include maps, photos, drawings and text.

- Make an **Environmental Palette**, select colours (paints or crayons) 'on location' to match features in the environment. Back in the classroom children can colour in their drawings.

How do I develop a geographical enquiry approach?

The Programmes of Study for Geography state that pupils should be given the opportunity **to undertake studies that focus on geographical questions, e.g. 'What/Where is it?', 'What is it like?', 'How did it get like this?', 'How and why is it changing?' KS1 1,6 & KS2 1,2,5**

Geographical enquiry is the process of asking questions about places to further the development of geographical understanding. The activities suggested in this guidance are based upon the idea that children learn most about their surroundings by asking questions. This is the process of geographical enquiry. Scientists enquire about objects, historians about time but in geography questions are always anchored to the environment. You will come across variations of the questions from the PoS in many different guises. These questions, and others like them, are useful because they can be applied to almost any locality or place that is the focus of children's enquiries and form a basis for comparing one locality with another.

Planning for geographical enquiries needs to be systematic - you will need to establish a clear route of enquiry, particularly if it involves work outside the classroom. Children should be encouraged to ask supplementary questions to the ones you pose.

An enquiry sequence involves:

Asking questions

↓

Gathering and Recording Data

↓

Communicating Information

Geographical enquiries can be undertaken at a variety of scales. The school grounds and the immediate environs would be the natural focus for key stage 1 enquiries. There are many questions that can be investigated in a very small area by asking 'What is it like?' You could generate activities based on the environmental qualities of the playground, you could investigate building materials or find out what children like and dislike about the school building.

At key stage 2, the scope of enquiries can be wider, both in terms of area and the complexity of geographical questions asked. Comparing the school locality with a contrasting UK locality could be based on the questions 'How did these places get like this?' and 'How and why are these places changing?'.

Geographical enquiries should use both primary (firsthand data collected by the children outside the classroom) and secondary (data gathered from books, speakers, etc.) sources of evidence.

Examples of a geographical enquiry planning sequence for both key stages 1 and 2 are shown in Figures 4 and 5. A blank version of this planner, for your own use, is given in the Appendices.The panel below outlines the sequence of preparation and follow up.

Planning your geographical enquiry

- Identify an issue and carry out your planning for a small-scale geographical enquiry, e.g. do we need a bench in the playground? OR

- Identify the steps that children would take to identify a suitable issue.

- Discuss the best way to collect information, the different kinds of information required, and how to collect the results.

- List the practical issues related to the process, such as equipment needed, the degree of supervision required.

- Decide what classroom preparation will be required.

- For each stage of the enquiry identify the resources that you have available, and those you need to find! Initially this can be quite time consuming, but it will make the enquiry run more smoothly. You may find materials to hand from enquiries in maths, science or history by other classes.

- Identify opportunities for follow-up geographical, literacy and numeracy activities, display, presentation and assessment.

- Identify strategies for differentiation so that everyone can take part and achieve.

GEOGRAPHICAL ENQUIRY PLANNING SHEET

Focus for enquiry: a visit to a farm – to find out what a farm is and what it does (Year 2)

Enquiry stage	Activities A selection chosen from...	PoS	Classroom preparation	Differentiation	Resources	Assessment from NC Level Descriptions
Identify **key questions** you would ask children to investigate.	Where is the farm? What type of place is it? What is it like? How are land and buildings used? (landuse) Where does food come from?	1c 1a 1b 5a 6a 5c 5d	Discuss what a farm is for. Find out the farm's location on a map. Plan journey, what clothes to wear, safety etc. Identify land use on a plan.	Different children will cope with fewer/more questions to think about and answer on the day.	Atlases/small scale maps of the region. Large scale maps of the farm.	Children....show an awareness of places beyond their own locality. Level 2 ....offer explanations for the location of features. Level 3
Identify *what* data needs to be collected and *how* it will be gathered.	Tour around farm using a map to follow a route. Mark features and landuse on map. Ask questions about: crops, animals, weather, buildings, jobs, machinery, output etc.	3b 3e 3d 1b 3a	Discuss how to colour code land use or how to use symbols on a map. Introduce appropriate geographical vocabulary. Prepare questions to ask.	Maps can be partially completed. Different levels of teacher support. Limit the number of tasks for some children.	Base maps of farm buildings and land. Talk by farmer. Worksheets looking at key questions.	...use their own observations to respond to questions about places. Level 2 ....use skills to respond to geographical questions. Level 3
Identify the ways in which the data will be interpreted.	Compare maps. Make neat copy (or whole -class wall version) of land use map using symbols/colours to identify features. Discuss farmer's views.	2 3d 3a	Organise small group tasks. Prepare a large-scale version of the farm plan.	Different tasks given to different ability groups. Tasks divided within groups.	Class map.	Children describe human and physical features of places. Level 2 ....offer reasons for their observations. Level 3
Identify how conclusions might be arrived at.	Compare different farms. Write stories about visit and their likes/dislikes. Answer key questions.	5b 6a	Use a photo pack of a contrasting farm. Refer back to key questions. Discuss the visit with a view to story writing.	Different responses and outcomes to key questions anticipated. Allow different forms of presentation e.g. oral.	Display space. Story books.	...express views about localities. Level 2 ....describe and make comparisons between different localities. Level 3

Figure 4: Geographical enquiry planning sheet: a key stage 1 example. A blank version of this planner is on page 58

GEOGRAPHICAL ENQUIRY PLANNING SHEET
Focus for enquiry: land use in a rural village (contrast to urban locality) Year 6 – two day project

Enquiry stage	Activities A selection chosen from...	PoS	Classroom preparation	Differentiation	Resources	Assessment
Identify key questions you would ask children to investigate.	Where is the village? What type of place is it? What is it like? How are land and buildings used? How did it get like this? How and why is the village changing?	1d 5e 1b 2a 5a 5c 5c 9b 9a 5d 9c	Discuss different types of settlement. Find the village's location. Plan journey, what clothes to wear, safety etc. Discuss village origins. Look at features on old plans.	Different children will cope with fewer/more questions to think about and answer on the day. More able can set their own questions to investigate.	Atlases/small scale maps of region. Large scale maps of the village. Secondary sources.	Pupils....offer explanations for the location of features. Level 3 ....begin to offer some explanations for the geographical patterns. Level 5
Identify what data needs to be collected and how it will be gathered.	**Children work in groups to cover different parts of the village.** Use a large scale map to follow a route around village. Mark land use on map. Identify changes to land use. Ask questionnaires.	3d 3c 3b 2b 3a	Introduce appropriate geographical vocabulary. Discuss how to colour code land use or how to use symbols on a map. Prepare questionnaires.	Maps can be blank or partially completed by the teacher. Different levels of teacher support. Limit number of tasks.	Village maps with route marked on. Blank base maps of the village to record land use. Worksheets looking at key questions.	...use skills and sources of evidence to respond to geographical questions. Level 3 ...select and use appropriate skills to investigate places. Level 5
Identify the ways in which the data will be interpreted.	Compare own maps with earlier maps of the village. Make composite map of land use. Tally responses to questionnaires.	2c 3e 3c 3f	Use maps at similar scales. Use other secondary sources of evidence e.g. photos. Organise small group tasks. Prepare a large scale version of the farm plan. Groups compare questionnaire results.	Different tasks given to different ability groups. Tasks divided within groups. Reduce/increase number of secondary data sources.	Photographs, maps and other evidence showing village in previous years.	...offer reasons for their observations and judgements about places. Level 3 ...offer explanations for the ways in which people affect the environment. Level 5
Identify how conclusions might be arrived at.	Answer key questions through:- Role play to investigate different views about changes in the village. Comparing village to school locality. Evaluate methods of enquiry.	3a 1b 2c 9c 5b	Refer back to key questions. Discuss the evidence with view to assuming roles. School locality may face similar changes - issues need to be identified.	Different responses and outcomes to key questions will be anticipated. Extra support in planning presentation.	Display space. Role cards to assist in role play.	...describe and make comparisons between different localities. Level 3 ...describe how processes lead to similarities and differences between places. Level 5

Figure 5: Geographical enquiry planning sheet: a key stage 2 example. A blank version of this planner is on page 58

6: Resourcing locality activities

Geographical information is readily available within any locality. There are many sources for local information: the local library, the commercial section of the local council which provides information for people coming into the town for business purposes, the local chamber of trade, the local history or reminiscence group/association, the free or other local press who should have an archive, the parish church, the local Ramblers' Association or walkers group. Most should be known to the local librarian who should be the first reference for titles, addresses and contact names.

Current planning information
County plans are available at the local library. These back up observations of changes and inform discussion about the reasons for change.

Historical evidence
Most large villages and small towns have been written about by an enthusiastic local historian. The post office, tourist information centre and local library often have these slim volumes. Figure 6 gives the advantages and requirements for working with collectable resources.

Maps
Using maps to investigate a locality
It would be impossible to make a geographical investigation of a locality without reference to maps. Children must be familiar with the language of maps if they are to take an active role in a locality study. Children should have been introduced to making and using simple maps and plans of familiar places (e.g. their classroom, the playground) at an early stage. Maps make most sense to children if they are an integral part of geographical investigations: combine using maps with observations, following a route, asking questions and recording data about how space is used. Maps should be used as a source of information and as a means of recording and displaying information.

Using maps ───────────► Making maps

Using maps		Making maps
• A source of information	• Recording information onto a base map	• Drawing a sketch map
• Locating places	• Using symbols and colours to represent features and values	• Measuring features and making a map from scratch
• Identifying locations of features		• Drawing maps of routes
• Using playmats		
• Following a route	• Showing ways in which land and buildings are used	• Making thematic maps to show how geographical features form patterns
• Using grid references		
• Working with scale, distance and direction		
• Comparing maps with aerial photographs		
• Identifying patterns on maps		

Time for fieldwork is often limited: it is important to be clear about which mapwork skills you want children to develop. Making maps from scratch is a valuable skill, but it does take a lot of time. For enquiry purposes, ready prepared base maps can be used to investigate, to record information, and to guide children around the locality. An example is given in Figure 7.

As children get more experienced they will be able to cope with more complex information on maps. They will also be able to design their own maps and be less reliant on the map data you provide. In follow-up work, completed maps are a useful tool to present the data children have collected and, for older children, to identify geographical patterns.

Making your base maps
Good sources of base maps are: school plans, tourist boards, local councils, planning departments, estate agents, local telephone directories, A-Z road maps. Most of these maps will be subject to copyright. This should be checked before you use them and acknowledged.

Source	Main advantages	Things to be aware of
Teachers' personal knowledge and experience	The information can be tailored to the focus of the study and pitched at the correct level for the children. The locality can be made 'real' with the use of anecdotes, visual aids and artefacts. More flexible planning.	It takes time to prepare and may not be easy to match up personal knowledge with 'geographical' activities. The responsibility for preparing activities lies with you.
Information centres	Topical and focused on the locality - lots of material usually available at a low cost. Can offer guidance for your planning and preparation. Some information centres have their own worksheets, such as town trails.	Centres need warning if a whole class is due to visit! The information may be biased to 'sell' the locality.
Firsthand accounts from other adults	Good source of oral histories and points of interest in the locality. The speakers do not have to be experts, and can bring personal perspectives to the study. Unusual artefacts and visual sources may be provided.	Needs careful preparation to ensure the talk is pitched at the right level and includes some geographical focus. Teachers will need time to liaise with the speaker to plan and prepare follow-up materials.
Photographs of the locality	A very flexible resource. It is easy to take snapshots of a wide range of geographical features which show both broad views and small details. Can be combined with aerial photographs and maps. Suitable for use by individuals and small groups. Children can choose and take the photos themselves.	Need to ensure a wide range of views. Should be the best quality possible so that detail is clearly seen. Photos can be wasted if they are not matched up to specific activities or questions. Several copies of each photo will allow them to be used for specific activities or questions.
Video of the locality	Can be a useful starting point for a study, in a format which children are used to viewing. Allows the whole class to view together with the teacher, stopping the video for discussion at appropriate points. Videos can be made by the school and swapped with one made by your twinned school.	Rarely available of the locality you have chosen, so will require planning and filming by teachers. Should be carefully scripted to include wide range of geographical features. Commercially made videos may not be appropriate, being designed to attract tourists or businesses.
Slides of the locality	Useful alternative to photographs which will allow whole class viewing and discussion. Easy to resource. Plan to have slides of the same views shown by some of the photographs.	You will need a good camera and quality slide film, as well as blackout facilities, to ensure the image is clear.
Books and stories	Textbooks and other adult books may provide factual information and illustrations. Local history books are useful as they often refer to small scale localities. A story book pitched at the children's level set in the locality is a great starting point, but these are rare.	Many books cover larger areas than the locality you are studying. Texts can often be too dense or weighty for children. It is better to select appropriate material in advance. You could write your own story book!
Local newspapers	Topical events can be studied through a library of cuttings. Provides different perspectives. Often a good source of local information and events. Some photographs may be useful. Cheap and up-to-date resource. Estate agents are another useful source.	Language and content may not be appropriate, particularly at KS1. May be biased or sensationalist in reporting events.
Commercially produced pack	Can reduce teachers' planning and preparation. Can offer suggestions and ideas which can be adapted to your own locality. Alternatively, resource packs can be produced and swapped between twinned schools in different localities.	Determines where the study takes place, rather than allowing you to choose the most appropriate locality.

Figure 6: Using different sources of information for UK locality studies

Figure 7a: Base map

Figure 7b: Base map with grid

Steps towards successful map making

- Make them clear — Make copies onto white paper with strong black outlines.
- Keep them simple — Take off unnecessary details (Tippex). Only show the area required.
- Make them manageable — Use A4 sheets on clipboards for easy handling outside.
- Use an appropriate version — Use a base map with a grid (Figure 7b) if location/position are key elements of the activity; use a base map without a grid (Figure 7a) to record land use or add information.

Style of map

Black and white outline maps are best for:
- recording data
- economy (cheaper to reproduce)
- black and white reproductions

Colour maps are best for:
- finding out a range of information
- colour reproduction (a lot of information is lost if colour maps are photocopied to b/w versions)

Choose maps which suit the activity. A street map shows .... roads! It does not show the spaces between roads at the correct scale and is unsuitable as a base map to record land use. But it is a good map to use if the children have to plan routes around a locality.

Scale

Full colour small-scale Ordnance Survey (OS) Landranger (1:50 000) and Pathfinder (1:25 000) maps set the context for a locality study. They cover a large area and show how a place is linked to other places by road, rail and river. Large scale black and white OS maps provide detail for a small area suitable for base maps. The characteristics of the different scales are shown in the panel below. The grid lines on each map are part of the National Grid (and often indicated on the better street maps). They are one kilometre apart and the numbering is the same regardless of map scale. Each square thus covers one square kilometre and has a unique number given from the numbers of the lines crossing in the bottom left hand (south west) corner. The number of the vertical line is given first, followed by the number of the horizontal line. This is the four figure grid reference for the square. Find the square for the school on maps of different scale. Draw the grid lines round the square at each scale and see how, as the square gets smaller so less detail is shown - the square 'shrinks' - a concept fully appreciated by six year olds used to playing with LEGO models.

The OS can print large-scale black and white maps to cover a specific location (e.g. your school and its immediate vicinity, a rural village centre or a part of a town). These prints are called Superplans or Site Centred Maps and are made using up to date digital map data. Most LEAs now have access to and a licence to copy digitised map data and offer a map service to schools; if not, contact your local OS agency (see page 56). OS maps are quite expensive at larger scales and involve a substantial initial outlay. However, they can be reproduced and used in a variety of situations as base maps and plans for investigating localities (Note: Local Authority schools have copyright licensing agreements through their LEA with the Ordnance Survey. Independent schools must make their own agreement with the Ordnance Survey who now have realistic fees for these schools).

Scale	Approximate land area shown on A4 extract	Possible use
1:50 000	10km x 14km	Colour large enough to show a city and suburbs
1:25 000	5km x 7km	Colour shows a town centre, open water and space
1:10 000	2km x 3km	B&W roughly catchment area size, many labels
1:5 000	1km x 1.5km	B&W covers a village
1:2 500	500m x 700m	B&W covers the local area around school
1:1 250	250m x 350m	B&W covers the school and its vicinity in great detail

Goad plans, which have been used to create the base maps of Ashbourne in Figure 7, are a very useful alternative to OS maps. Goad plans are black and white, show the outlines of buildings and are produced for every town and shopping centre in the country. They are at an appropriate scale for locality studies and can be adapted for many different purposes. They are produced with or without shop names and details (see Figures 7 and 12). The plain Ashbourne map has been given a grid by overlaying a grid copied onto clear acetate and then recopied. Grids for this purpose are provided in the Appendices.

Photographs

Photographs are an essential part of locality studies at every stage. They enable you to:
- gain an impression of the locality before you visit it
- compare the map of the locality with an aerial photograph
- show the children features of a locality which they can find on a trail
- record features in the locality

- display information gathered during fieldwork
- present and communicate ideas once the enquiry is over

Quality is important. Ensure that the images given to children are clear and can be 'read'. The younger the child, the larger and more selective the picture. Have a sufficient number of images for children to look at and use colour photographs wherever possible. Borrow a video camera, with the owner as helper too, to promote your good work through moving images. Video images are an excellent way of exchanging information with a school in your contrasting locality and can incorporate all the points mentioned above in making a collection. For each school and class this strategy also covers the need to make balanced studies for an interested audience.

Photographs can be used in a variety of different ways:
- to develop children's geographical vocabulary

Photo: Paula Richardson

- to ask and answer geographical questions
- to record images in a non-verbal way
- to communicate ideas and information

Photographs can be used at every stage of the enquiry process. Postcard views provide first impressions of a locality before you visit it. On the visit collect as many postcards of the locality as possible and use as part of an initial display both for your INSET and for starting the enquiry process.

Compare the map of the locality with an aerial photograph for added dimension. This assists the recognition of patterns for further investigation. Aerial photographs are getting cheaper and you can select images easily. It is not essential to use professionally produced materials, ordinary snaps are fine. Images taken from the top of flats, offices and other high buildings often relate to views the children have seen. Using these helps them make sense of their surroundings.

A range of photographs is vital. Take and use images of broad views and small features: i.e. photograph at different scales. This emphasises the relationship of detail to the main features of the environment. View from different directions, for example, from either end of a street, and from different perspectives, for example, from ground level then from the rooftops. Show human and natural features, include people and their activities. Show different types and ages of building, open space and the effect of slope on the buildings and views. Collect images at different times of the day, for example, rush hour, mid-afternoon, and at different times of the year, for example, sunny, wet, snowy days.

This collection, made on preparation visits or via a twinned school, can be used to show features in the locality for children to find on a trail when preparing their initial investigation. Mount these and other photographs taken during the 'reconnoitre' onto a large version of a map to draw attention to features which merit discussion when sorting out an enquiry issue.

Let children choose and take images (simple cameras, even throwaway ones, fulfil IT requirements) and continue to collect as part of their information gathering processes in the field. For example, provide photographic evidence of 'busy' and 'quiet', 'nice' and 'nasty'. Mount photographs in sequence to illustrate the route followed or survey made - this might be a row of shops or houses or evidence of erosion and deposition in a stream. Add speech bubbles to an image of people in the locality to express their likes and dislikes discovered through interview. This could be the children themselves or local people.

Once the enquiry is complete the photographs are an essential part of presenting and communicating ideas. Mount a photograph on a large sheet of paper so that geographical questions, labels and descriptions using geographical vocabulary can be written around the outside. Children can work in pairs. Each child can write questions around a mounted photograph. These can be exchanged so that children can find answers to each other's questions from the photograph.

Photographs can form part of an assessment exercise. Get children to select a range of images to represent a locality on a postcard, or choose just one photograph that sums up feelings or the character of a locality. Finally, match descriptions of geographical features to a range of photographs.

Information Technology

A locality study provides many opportunities to integrate IT in a meaningful way, through using real data that the children have collected during their fieldwork. The IT competences required by the National Curriculum can be covered as follows:
Handling information, e.g.
- Collecting, recording and displaying survey results.
- Using computer generated maps to look at changes in the locality.
  Controlling, monitoring and modelling, e.g.

- Designing a plan for a new shopping centre, using a 3-D map package to display ideas.
- Using simple weather-monitoring software to investigate micro-climates in the locality.

Examples of uses of IT are shown in Figure 8. The most useful software for geographical purposes is the open ended, generic software which comes with most platforms. There are packages which come with additional files of data to allow pupils to practise manipulation of data before entering data collected by the school survey and measurement. There are a few CD-ROMs which can be used with care to provide the basis for detailed work in particular localities (see page 56).

Data collected on a simple survey were entered upon a spreadsheet and used to compare features of the local area with the contrasting locality (Figure 9). For further information on surveys and data handling see page 39.

Designing tally charts to record data collected during surveys.	Using spreadsheets and databases to retrieve, sort and analyse data.	Using spreadsheet data to draw graphs and pie charts.
Recording information collected into prepared databases.	**Opportunities for Information Technology**	Making maps and plans using computer simulations.
Writing letters to interested parties about field work findings.	Desk top publishing displays and presentations	Communicating and sharing data with other schools (fax, e-mail).

Figure 8: Opportunities for Information Technology

Name	Where do you live?	Favourite place	Favourite building	Favourite shop	Favourite activity
Jamie	Heaton Moor	Heaton Moor Park	The Old Bakers	Spar	Riding my bike
Helena	Heaton Moor	Don't know	The Co-op Pyramid office	Bay Tree	Going shopping
Mushtaq	Heaton Mersey	Heaton Common	The Sports Centre	None	Going to the common
Sophie	Heaton Moor	Heaton Moor	Heaton Moor Shops	Bay Tree	Playing with my friends

We did a survey of our favourite places and swapped it with our twin school. They sent us their favourite places on a floppy disk. This is the survey we did.

Figure 9: Some of the data from a class survey

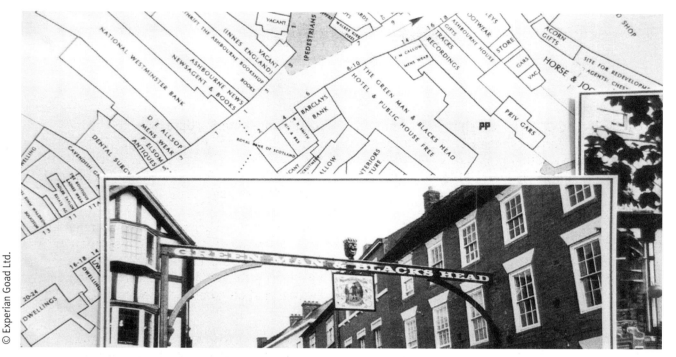

Display material

The visual and graphical content of material gathered and analysed automatically lends itself to wall and table display. The sense of place is enhanced when the photographs and maps are also shown alongside artefacts of food (labels), clothes, commercial products, newspaper articles, and stories set in the locality. Displays can grow from early photographs to which are added increasing evidence of character through detailed photographs and the children's work on maps and graphs. Descriptions and commentary can be added from other presentations.

Communicating the results

Presentations are a useful way for children to communicate their findings. They offer many opportunities to assess children's ability to meet the expectations of level in geography, and also the requirements of the English PoS to identify the range of speaking, listening, reading and writing expected at different key stages. They give children a focus for talking about real issues to different audiences and a chance to demonstrate their use of geographical vocabulary.

The great variety possible is shown in Figure 10.

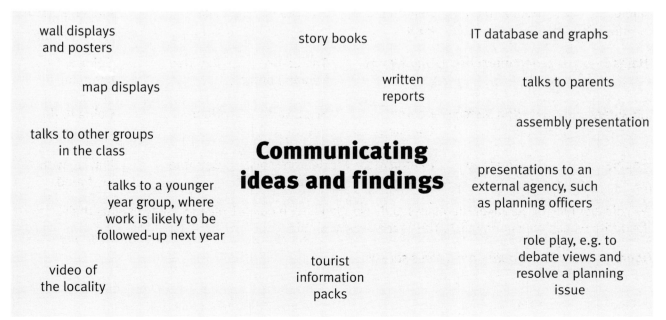

wall displays and posters

story books

IT database and graphs

map displays

written reports

talks to parents

talks to other groups in the class

Communicating ideas and findings

assembly presentation

talks to a younger year group, where work is likely to be followed-up next year

presentations to an external agency, such as planning officers

video of the locality

tourist information packs

role play, e.g. to debate views and resolve a planning issue

Figure 10: Communicating ideas and findings

7: Locality activities

Planning activities

The aim of all learning activities in geography is to integrate the three elements of geography: skills, places and themes. The child's knowledge and understanding of a place can be increased by looking at thematic aspects of the place whilst developing skills of observation, recording, analysis and evaluation. The usual medium is maps, the unique tools of the geographer, but this can also be done via other means of graphical explanation which enhance basic skills used elsewhere in the curriculum.

The activities which follow have been linked to relevant sections of the PoS and typical geographical questions that you could use as a focus for children's investigations. You can adapt these elements according to the place you investigate and check overall coverage of the PoS using the grid in the Appendices. The ideas will also develop learning in other areas of the curriculum, such as language skills, maths and graphicacy, art, technology and social skills. Links are suggested in the notes.

The activities described address the three key elements of skills, places, and themes. Figure 11 relates the activities to key geographical questions and the fieldwork framework.

Putting the locality into context
The PoS for geography **KS1 and KS2 1c**
This is the stage preceding fieldwork when work aims to identify where the locality is in relation to other places.

Geographical enquiry focus questions: Where is this place? What type of place is it?

You can introduce this stage by asking children to tell you what they already know about the locality, from firsthand knowledge or from other sources. Start with where the locality is in relation to the school and their homes, then find the locality on maps of different scales. Start by looking in an atlas, then use the local small-scale maps (Landranger and Pathfinder); finally

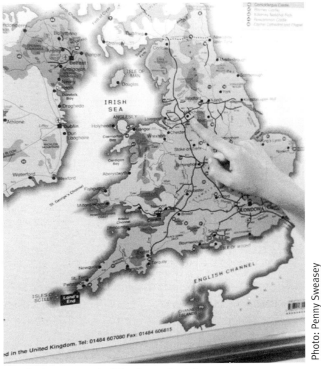
Photo: Penny Sweasey

study large-scale black and white maps (OS 1:10 000 or street maps). Use the National Curriculum maps to mark the location of the place. Use an atlas map to find out what county the locality is part of. Find out what links the locality has with other places: is it on a main road or rail route? Relate these findings to UK maps of road and rail links in the front of most school atlases. Add the findings to the simple National Curriculum UK map.

Meet visiting speakers, perhaps inviting in people who know or use the locality you will be studying.

Make contact with a link school to share and swap information about their school localities.

Begin to describe features in comparison to those of their own area.
(see Wallace, G. (1995) 'Your place or mine?' *Primary Geographer*, Jan)

Do these activities before you study any locality, to give children a greater sense of understanding in their fieldwork activities.

Question	Some possible activities/skills	Main resources
Where is it?	Planning a journey Putting into context	Atlas, road atlas, and large-scale OS maps
What is the place like?	Description: Observation trail, make presentation	Photographs, video
Why is it like that?	Analysis: Interpreting surroundings, observation trail, create display	Surveys and sketches, photographs, weather data
What is the landscape like?	Comparison with own locality Observation trail, sketching	Photographs, sketches
What goods and services are available there?	Let's go shopping Land-use mapping Add to display	Lists of everyday and special needs
Where do people go to shop?	Make 'signpost map' with distance and direction	Map, photographs, road atlases
What work do the adults do?	Prepare job advertisements for area Collect evidence of local products	Photographs, survey, video, interviews
How do people travel?	Analysis: linking methods of travel to reasons for travelling	Information about locality, newspapers, small-scale maps, photographs
What is it like to live there?	Empathy: 'A day in the life of....' Interviews with local people Built and physical environment activities	Information about locality, newspapers, surveys, photographs
What links does it have with other places?	Identification of global nature of places Locate destination of product	OS maps, globe, road and other atlases
What is the weather like there?	Prepare and present a weather forecast for locality Exchange faxes Data from micro-climate observations	Weather data (from daily newspapers), photographs, data from locality of school
How is the place changing?	Collect evidence of change Identify locations on map Display evidence	Local newspaper, photographs
Why is it changing?	Discussion: who will benefit from changes being made?	Information about locality from interview and observations
How do the people feel about the changes?	Role play Enquiry and interviews Complete display	Information about locality from interview and observations
How is the locality similar to our locality and other localities we have studied?	Comparison: create list of similarities and differences in written or pictorial form	Using previous knowledge, photographs

Figure 11: The relationship of activities to geographical questions

Geographical skills: Using maps, planning fieldwork, making comparisons, recognising patterns, describing features, increasing awareness, using secondary sources, using geographical vocabulary, asking questions.

Geographical vocabulary: Locality, place, site, map, scale, landmark, direction, features, address, local, near, far, route, urban, rural, village, town, city, county, country, UK.

Links with other subjects:
English: Speaking and listening
History: The local area

Land-use mapping activities

The PoS for geography **key stage 1, make and use maps and plans (3d, 3e); investigate how land and buildings are used (5d). Key stage 2 develop the ability to recognise and explain patterns (1c); understand how 'the features of the localities influence the nature and location of human activities within them' (5c); investigate how land in settlements is used in different ways (9b).**

Geographical enquiry focus questions: What are land and buildings in this locality used for? What do people do in this place?

The aim of this activity is to record the different land uses in the locality on a base map or a Goad Plan (see Figure 7). With the children, devise a key to represent the main land use types in the area. This would be a simple picture key for younger children but symbols and colour codes can be introduced to older children (see Figure 12). Categorise buildings and spaces into those where people work, live, spend their leisure time, provide services and so on.
Look at the types of land use which have been mapped. Discuss with the children the activities that people do in the different places and how these places seem to be grouped making patterns of land use. Try to find explanations for land-use patterns. Aerial views (perhaps from a tall building) are a useful source for explaining

the patterns, understood even by young children.

After the initial survey it may be possible to classify shops. Suggested categories are: what they sell, size (single storey or having several floors for selling), having a car park for shoppers, being part of a shopping mall. Houses can be classified according to type: terraced, semi-detached, detached, flats, maisonettes. With older children other buildings can be classified according to age, function, height, style. Different ways of recording and presenting results can be explored: sketching, graphs, wall displays, pie charts/bar charts, 3-D modelling.

Investigate whether the shape of the land affects the way the land is used. Is the land use on flat land similar to or different from that on sloping land or on hills? How is the land used next to the river?

Street names, old building names and fading signs painted on the sides of buildings can be investigated: they may present clues about previous land use or the origins of buildings.

SHOP	COLOUR
Food	[ ]
Clothes	[ ]
Shoes	[ ]
Supermarket	[ ]
Electrical	[ ]
Games/toys	[ ]
Papers/books	[ ]
Jewellery	[ ]
Pots/pans	[ ]
Places to eat	[ ]
Others	[ ]

Figure 12: A simple land use key

Geographical skills: Using fieldwork skills and equipment, using observation, recognising patterns, describing features, using geographical vocabulary, taking photographs, making maps with symbols, communicating ideas.

Geographical vocabulary: Land use, buildings, houses, factories, shops, site, symbols, represent, street, office, transport, car park, open spaces, activity, leisure, services, recreation, employment, residential, settlement.

Links with other subjects:
Maths: Classifying and representing data.
Design and Technology: Modelling.

Observation trails
The PoS for geography **use appropriate geographical terms and vocabulary (3a); follow routes on a map (3e/d).**

Geographical enquiry focus questions: What is this place like? How do you feel about this locality?

Select an area which is safe and which has scope for a range of exploratory activities. Plan a short route through the area which incorporates sites for activities at intervals along the route. Plot the route on a base map with an overlaid grid. At its simplest this can be a straightforward walk with stops to take a photograph, look at and discuss a feature, answer questions, or carry out activities - perhaps with the photos (see page 26).

You could, however, devise an 'Observation Trail': a treasure hunt, a guide to the locality or a story board for a TV programme, using clues to study the detail and function of an area. Observation trails encourage children to observe, explore and investigate. They can look at a whole range of features or just one: for example, building materials, shop fronts, names and writing in the environment, or different surface textures. You could devise a Sensory

Walk worksheet with cards to encourage close observation, as in Figure 13.

Other activities draw attention to detail by colour or name (Rainbow and Alphabet I-Spy); or to people who live in the locality and use its services (Different People and Let's Go Shopping)(see Figure 14).

The children could use their observations to make a video of the locality to send to their twinned school.

Geographical skills: Using observation, using maps to follow routes and directions, describing features, using geographical vocabulary, increasing awareness, taking photographs.

Geographical vocabulary: Features, views, attractive, ugly, interesting, environment, trails, routes, co-ordinates, grid square, location, zone.

Links with other subjects:
Art: Recording images.
English: Writing and Communicating.
History: Local area.

The built environment
Pupils should investigate **the human and physical features that give a place its character (5a), the attractive and unattractive features of an environment (6a), and how the environment can be improved and sustained (6c). Plus at KS2 how people affect the environment (10a).**

Geographical enquiry focus questions: Do you like this place? Is it a good environment? How do people spoil the environment?

Draw attention to building features, and building materials and other aspects of the environment by voting on the class's favourite buildings and the reasons for choosing them (Figure 15). Survey street furniture looking at its purpose and efficiency, its design compatibility with the environment, and ways of improving it.

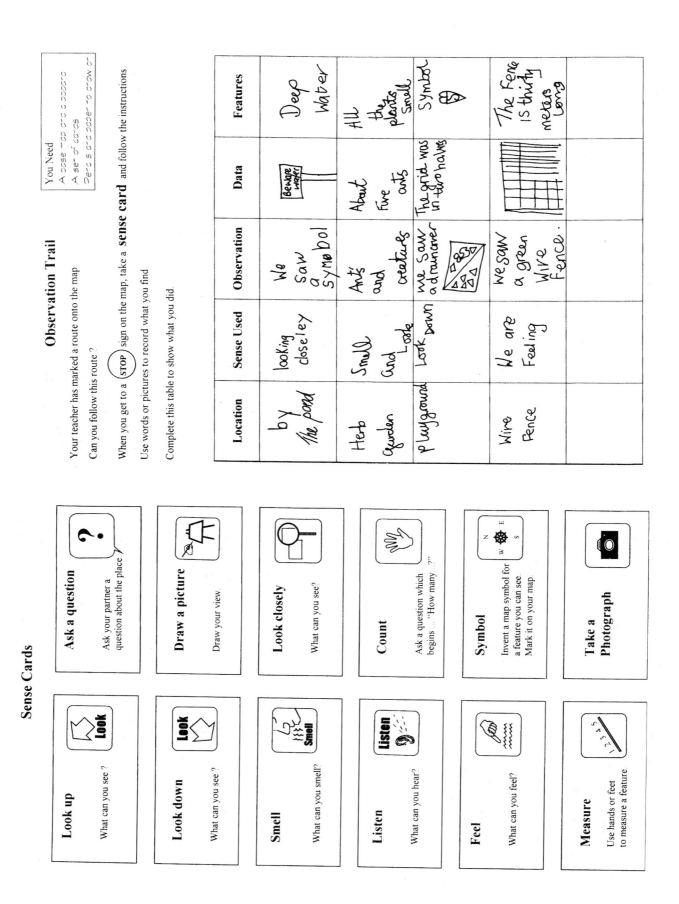

Observation Trail

You Need
A close ⌐⊐ ⌐⊐ ⌐ ⌐⊐⊐⌐⊐
A ser ⊐⌐ ⌐⌐⌐⊐
⊐⌐⊐ ⌐ ⌐⊐ ⊐⊐⊐⌐⌐ ⊐ ⌐⊐⌐ ⌐⌐

Your teacher has marked a route onto the map.

Can you follow this route?

When you get to a (STOP) sign on the map, take a **sense card** and follow the instructions.

Use words or pictures to record what you find

Complete this table to show what you did

Location	Sense Used	Observation	Data	Features
by the pond	looking closely	We saw a symbol	Beware water	Deep Water
Herb garden	Smell and Look	Ants and creatures	About five ants	All these plants Small Symbol
Playground	Look down	we saw a draincover	The grid was in two halves	
Wire Fence	We are Feeling	We saw a green Wire Fence.		The Fence is thirty meters long

Sense Cards

Ask a question
Ask your partner a question about the place.

Draw a picture
Draw your view.

Look closely
What can you see?

Count
Ask a question which begins .... "How many....?"

Symbol
Invent a map symbol for a feature you can see
Mark it on your map

Take a Photograph

Look up
What can you see ?

Look down
What can you see ?

Smell
What can you smell?

Listen
What can you hear?

Feel
What can you feel?

Measure
Use hands or feet to measure a feature.

Figure 13: A sensory walk

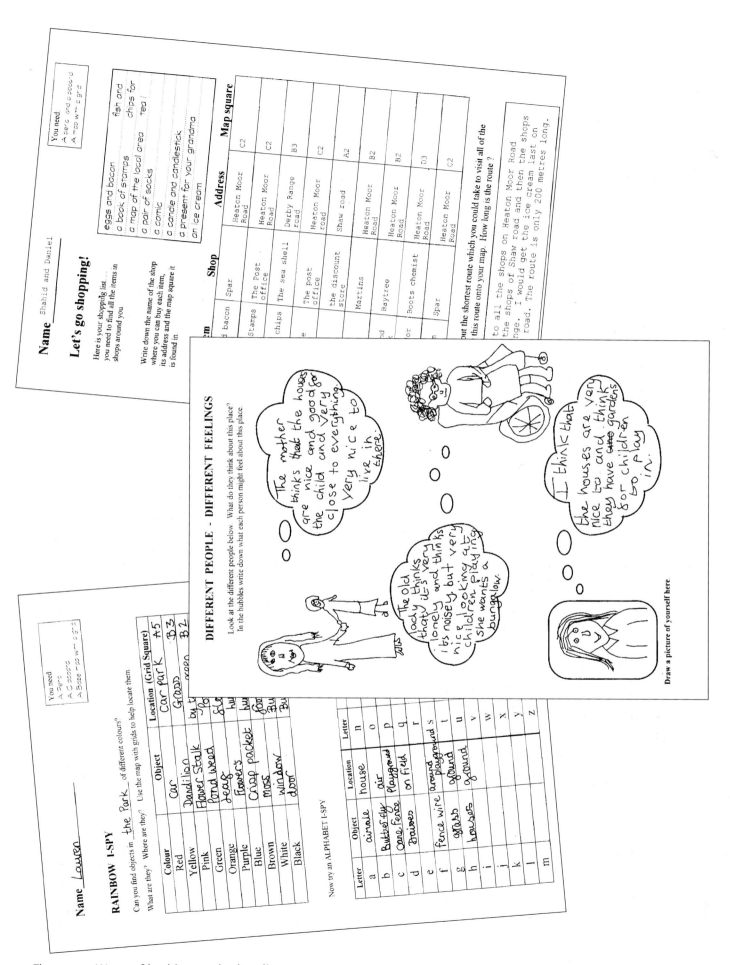

Figure 14: Ways of looking at the locality

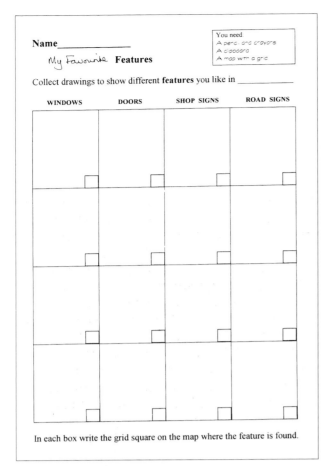

Figure 15: Draw attention to building features

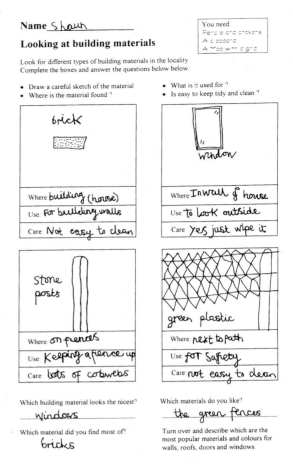

Figure 16: Looking at building materials

Observation techniques can be selected to allow for progression and to enable children to work at different levels of ability. Make wax crayon rubbings of surface textures; provide viewing and drawing frames (on acetate or graph paper) to encourage spatial observation; use magnifying glasses to clarify photograph and map details.

Writing poems encourages children to think about using a wide vocabulary to describe places and builds in opportunities for children to compare likes and dislikes and offer reasons for their choices.

Investigate how people have had a good or bad effect on the environment by looking for links between human activity and the quality of the environment. This may involve looking at recent changes in shop size and traffic use.

Investigate natural materials in the built environment, such as, rocks, water and vegetation. Investigate whether there is a link between the local geology and building materials (see Figure 16).

Geographical skills: Using fieldwork skills, using observation, making comparisons, sketching, using geographical vocabulary, increasing awareness, taking photographs, communicating ideas.

Geographical vocabulary: Any words related to description and evaluation of geographical environments such as, like, dislike, materials, style, texture, colours.

Links with other subjects:
Art: Visual perception, recording images, using media.
English: Whole range of language skills, verbal and written.

The physical environment
Pupils should be given opportunities to **investigate the effect of weather on people and their surroundings KS1 (5c), how weather varies between places and how site conditions can affect the weather. KS2 (8a), and about seasonal weather patterns (8b).**

Geographical enquiry focus questions: How do physical features give this place its character? What is the weather like in this place? How does the weather affect what people do here?

1. Follow the route on the map
2. At each dot on the map decide if the place is
   - windy
   - sunny
   - sheltered
3. When you have been to each place, decide where to put
   - a bench for people to sit on
4. Say why you chose your place

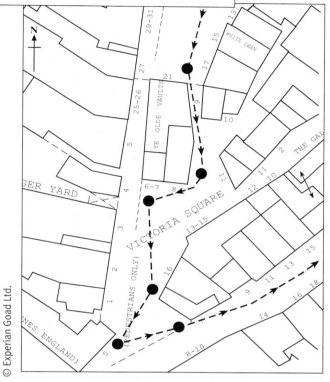

© Experian Goad Ltd.

Figure 17: 'Climate' in town

A good way to start is to investigate facilities provided for shelter in the playground by asking the children to choose the best place for different activities (such as eating lunch or playing different games) in different weather conditions and at different seasons. The different sites can be used to explore micro-climates using wind meters, thermometers and rain gauges, and the measurements can be used as evidence for planning 'best locations' for seats and flower tubs. Relate the findings to compass direction, the position of the sun and the presence or absence of sheltering walls and vegetation to develop further understanding. Older children can progress to consider the way that different parts of the locality have different 'climates' (for example, sunny spots, windy corners) and use the information to investigate 'what is the best location for ... a bench for shoppers / a bus shelter / a memorial garden / a weather vane etc.? (see Figure 17).

If you visit a site more than once you can investigate the effects of seasons on activities in a locality, for example, in a National Park, do people do different things at various times of the year? Collect evidence of changes during rainy weather, either by visiting on wet days or by testing in the classroom and playground what happens to water as it falls on different surfaces. Using different materials such as sand, clay, slate, concrete, grass, plant filled flower beds, helps children to understand larger phenomena. Compare how sudden flooding occurs in concrete-covered urban environments with how rain soaks into land left in a natural state. Discuss the needs of farmers and water boards for the land to act as a natural reservoir.

Rivers are a theme in key stage 2 (Para 7). Children need opportunities to look at how rivers shape the land. Is the river a feature of a settlement? Does it help make a defensive site? Ask questions such as 'Why was the castle built here?' or 'Is the river an attractive feature of this place?' Compare rivers or streams in the contrasting locality to a stream you visit in the local area. Find out about local floods and their effects on the local area. Severe weather conditions are recorded in local papers and these can be researched in any local library. Even if a school visit to the contrasting locality is not possible the local library can be asked to provide material suitable for fact-finding research.

Geographical skills: Using fieldwork skills and equipment, making comparisons, recognising patterns, looking at cause and effect, using geographical vocabulary, using geographical measuring equipment, making maps.

Geographical vocabulary: Weather, seasons, temperature, windy, shade, shelter, location, micro-climate, conditions, puddle, predictions, forecast, landscape, river, valley, slope, hill.

Links with other subjects:
Maths/Science: Using measuring and recording instruments.

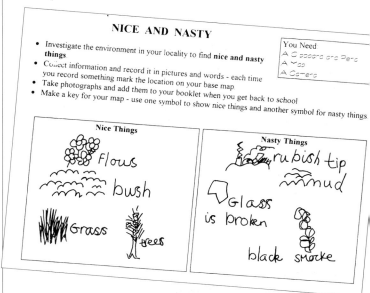

Figure 18: Is the environment cared for?

Environmental quality investigations

The PoS for geography states that pupils should **investigate the quality of the environment in a locality (KS1 6a, 6c) (KS2 10a, 10b)**.

Geographical enquiry focus questions: Is the quality of the environment good or bad? How do people affect the environment? How can we improve the environment?

The simple techniques used to investigate pollution as an environmental issue in science are given a further dimension in geography. Litter can be located, categorised, counted, graphed and the findings illustrated on a base map to give a geographical context to the work. The graphs will show how different kinds of litter are a problem in different parts of the community. Use the results and the map to communicate your findings to the local authority and to suggest ways to clean up the environment.

Tape recorders can be used to capture the different sounds and noises in a locality: show the noisy and quiet zones on a base map and use this information to make decisions about locating different features (for example, where is the best place for a hospital, which needs a quiet location?).

Traffic flows are indicators of levels of pollution in an area. Use base maps to record counts of different traffic types at different times. Look at the effects of pollution on people, buildings and activities.

Investigate whether an environment is 'cared for' by looking for evidence of poor maintenance and decay and record this with annotated field sketches and photographs (see Figure 18).

Look for evidence of 'green awareness' such as recycling bins. Map their location and decide whether they are optimally sited.

Geographical skills: Using fieldmaps, survey sheets and measuring equipment, using observation, making comparisons, recognising patterns, looking at cause and effect, identifying issues, asking questionnaires, making maps with symbols.

Geographical vocabulary: Environment, quality, care, improvement, traffic, litter, pollution, noise, rubbish, waste, recycle.

Links with other subjects:
Science: Experimental and investigative work, Health and safety.

Surveys and data handling

In key stage 2 pupils should have the opportunity to **use Information Technology to gain access to additional information sources and to assist in handling, classifying and presenting evidence (3f).**

Geographical enquiry focus question: What is happening here?

Identify an issue which you could investigate using a simple survey (i.e. collecting, counting and using data). Choose the survey area according to the age of children. Some suggestions are: landuse on a farm, the number of pedestrians on different routes, amount of traffic travelling in different directions.

Discuss the ways of collecting data and design a survey sheet or questionnaire or tally sheet. Safety must be a primary concern, but you will also need to consider what form the data will take and if it is easy to record.

Carry out the survey until you feel children have collected sufficient data to draw some broad conclusions. Illustrate the results on a base map to give a geographical focus to the activity, using shading to show values or drawing pictograms onto the map.

Use IT applications such as EXCEL, GRASS, DATASWEET and POINT to classify and present the findings (on spreadsheets, pie charts, bar graphs). Some children will be able to use their results to identify and explain geographical patterns (see Figure 19).

Geographical skills: Using fieldwork skills and equipment, using observation, making comparisons, recognising patterns, using geographical measuring equipment, predicting, testing, communicating ideas.

Geographical vocabulary: Survey, data, tally chart, questionnaire, chart, calculate, observe, predict, testing, activities, services, patterns, movement, journeys.

Links with other subjects:
IT/Maths: Communicating and handling/classifying data.

Location	Time	Cars	Buses	Lorries and Vans	Pedestrians
Heaton Moor Road	0 - 5 minutes	18	0	5	12
	5 - 10 minutes	23	2	7	26
	10 - 15 minutes	21	1	2	15
	15 - 20 minutes	29	0	8	24

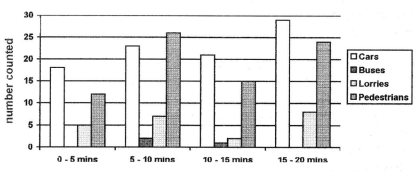

Figure 19: Spreadsheet and graph from traffic survey data

Photo: Penny Sweasey

Changing building functions - an extended project

This is an example of an activity which could be updated by successive year groups revisiting the locality.

The PoS for geography states that pupils should **investigate how the environment is changing, find out about recent or proposed changes in the locality and about particular issues arising from the way land is used (KS1 3f, 5d, 6b, 6c)(KS2 3e, 5c, 5d, 9c, 10a).**

Geographical enquiry focus questions:
How did this place get like this?
How and why is this place changing?

The first stage is for you to identify a 'space' or building in the locality which can be the focus for the children's investigation (see Figure 20). There are four possibilities:

1 A site which is derelict and has been unused for several years.

2 A site with potential for development, such as an under-used club house, gardens or bowling green.

3 A site which has changed function in recent times, such as an abandoned petrol station.

4 A building which has become run down and uncared for, such as a theatre, old cinema, or redundant place of worship.

Next draw a sketch of the building, annotating features (old and new) which give clues about: a. previous use or function, b. current function, c. major changes to structure or environment.

Finally, identify ways in which children could find out what it was like before: for example, from maps, photographs, parents, or older people who have lived locally for some time. Discuss children's ideas of why the changes have occurred and see if further research would be a good idea. If there are several sites to look at these could be plotted on a simple map.

Name _____	Changing Functions	You need:

Changing Functions

Investigate the locality to find out if it is changing. Use an old map to see if the land use has changed. Show the new buildings and label your drawings.

You need:
A pencil and clipboard
An old map of the place you are investigating

Old function or 'Before'	Grid square	New function or 'After'
The old Hospital	F4	New site for Business Park

Figure 20: Changing functions

Photos: Penny Sweasey

The second stage involves making plans for a new use for one site. Draw a sketch of the site, showing how you would redevelop and fill the space, and why. Then make a more accurate map of the site, if necessary tracing and enlarging boundaries from an OS map or Goad plan. Younger children need larger base maps to accommodate their larger printing. Show how the site might be re-developed, giving reasons for the choices made. Children should think about which groups of people might be in favour or opposed to their proposals. This would be an ideal opportunity to use role play in the classroom. It would be a good idea to involve the local community and the local planning offices. Children could be encouraged to write letters and plan visits from and to outside agencies.

Geographical skills: Using observation, making comparisons, looking at cause and effect, increasing awareness, identifying issues, using secondary and historical sources, communicating ideas.

Geographical vocabulary: Buildings, function, site, change, compare, redevelop, improve, run-down, derelict, heritage, planning, issues, conservation, restore.

Links with other subjects:
History: of the local area.

Photo: Paula Richardson

A safety survey

The following activity is an example of how geography leads into cross-curricular activities and addresses the wider curriculum, involving children in social issues (KS1 6a,6c) (KS2 5e,9e).

Geographical enquiry focus question: Is this a safe environment for ...?
Consider the needs of a particular group of people (such as small children, people with disabilities, older people) and identify the features which can make a place, or a building, or a route, unsafe for the group. Mark onto a base map the safe and unsafe areas, using red circles for dangerous places and blue rectangles

for safe places. Inside the circles and rectangles identify the hazard or safety feature (see Figure 21). This can be an opportunity to devise symbols. The activity is a good opportunity to involve Health and Safety Officers from the planning department of your local council.

Geographical skills: Using fieldwork skills and equipment, using observation, describing features, looking at cause and effect, increasing awareness, identifying issues, making maps with symbols, communicating ideas.

Geographical vocabulary: Safety, hazards, dangerous, needs, symbols, key, access, barrier.

Links with other subjects:
Science: Experimental and investigative work, health and safety.

Photo: Penny Sweasey

Name _Zoe_

A Safety Survey of _The Shopping Centre_

- Investigate the locality to see if it is a safe place. Look for things which make the place dangerous for people (these are called hazards). Look for things which make the place safe.

  A broken pavement could trip people up — this is a hazard.
  A Zebra crossing makes it safe to cross the road — this is a safety feature.

- Find out where the hazards and safe places are on your map.
- Invent a map symbol for each hazard and each safety feature.
- Draw the symbols for each hazard or safety feature on your map in the correct place.

Colour the circles red and draw your map symbols for hazards

1. a dangerous crossing
2. broken pavement
3. bin bags on the path
4. broken glass
5. a dark alley at night
6. steps might be slippery

Colour the squares blue and draw your map symbols for safety features

A — a zebra crossing
B — the lollipop lady
C — signs on the glass door
D — cone saying 'wet floor'
E — a play creche
F — ramp for pushchairs

When you get back to your classroom you can compare your map with your friends - did you find the same things?

Figure 21: A safety survey

8: Planning for progression and assessment

Developing knowledge and skills

The planning sheets (Figures 4 and 5) are examples of how key stage 1 and 2 plans for UK locality studies might look in practice. Progression is built in by increasing the range and complexity of geographical questions, skills and contexts. Progression is also achieved by planning locality studies with a view to the range of assessment objectives incorporated.

When planning your UK locality studies, be aware of the expectations for attainment described in the National Curriculum Level Descriptions. Plan opportunities for achievement, by matching the task to the desired outcome. You should plan for consistency and continuity across key stages 1 and 2, so that it is possible to chart children's progress in different aspects of geography.

The strands to incorporate in your assessment planning for UK locality studies are:

- **using geographical enquiry and skills**
- **knowledge and understanding of places**

These are the dominant strands but there is no reason why the others:

- **pattern and processes**
- **environmental issues**

should not feature too.

When children are working on a locality study, you will be able to assess them at three key points in the process: 1) in classroom preparation, 2) in work outside the classroom (fieldwork), and 3) in the evaluation and feedback stage.

SCAA have produced materials relating to the geography curriculum and assessment:
> *Expectations in Geography at Key Stages 1 and 2*
> *Geography at KS2 Curriculum Planning Guidance for Teachers*
> *Geography and the Use of Language at Key Stages 1 and 2*

It is advisable to consult the SCAA publications which contain exemplars from children's work. However, for immediate use the levels of expectation are in Figure 23 (pages 46-47).

Four aspects of geography, (places, patterns and processes, environmental relationships and issues and the ability to enquire and use geographical skills) can be identified within the Level Descriptions and relate to Para 1 in each of the key stage PoS. In the preceding table the expectations at the end of Year 2 relate to Level 2 in the context of key stage 1 PoS; at the end of year 4 to Level 3, and the end of Year 6 to Level 4, in the context of key stage 2 PoS.

Opportunities for assessment in these stages include:

Classroom preparation	Fieldwork	Evaluation and feedback
Groupwork and co-operation	Groupwork and co-operation	Groupwork and co-operation
Discussion skills	Safety awareness	Evidence of increased
Investigation using secondary sources	Enjoyment and participation	understanding
Asking geographical questions	Independence in data collection and recording skills	Analysis and conclusions
Using geographical language	Completion of set tasks	IT data handling
Independence in identifying tasks and methods	Observation skills	Quality of presentation
	Mapwork skills	Vocabulary learnt and used
		Communication skills

A step-by-step approach to planning

A medium term planning sequence (below) illustrates the stages to be carried out after devising a whole-school plan (as in Figure 3) and before planning the details of an actual enquiry (as in Figures 4 and 5). Drawing up a medium term plan could usefully form part of an INSET activity.

1 Match the curriculum aims to the possible locality activities

Look at the geography Programme of Study for the appropriate key stage.

Decide when the UK locality study activities can best take place within the whole school curriculum plan.

2 Decide on the place or locality you want to investigate

Consider: What is a suitable starting point? Which geographical themes or skills can be developed? Is the focus to be wholly geographical or will it have cross-curricular elements? Will there be opportunities for collecting data and using IT? (This stage may mean some reconsideration of the whole school plan.)

3 Will it be possible to visit the locality you have chosen?

Consider: the age of the children, distance, cost, safety, staffing and helpers, travel arrangements and contingency plans for bad weather.

4 Design a geographical enquiry

Identify questions based on the locality chosen and on the basis of available resources e.g. Where? What? Why? How? Who? When?

Design activities which can be used to investigate the locality and answer questions.

5 Which parts of the PoS have been covered?

KS1	1a,b,c	2	3a,b,c,d,e,f	4	5a,b,c,d	6				
KS2	1a,b,c	2a,b,c	3a,b,c,d,e,f	4	5a,b,c,d,e	6	7a,b	8a,b,c	9a,b,c	10a,b

6 Devise activities to include preparation and follow-up work

Consider: Displays and cross-curricular work. Plan assessment. Adapt activities according to the age and ability of the children.

7 Collect resources

Organise maps, photographs and other resources for the study, such as statistics, tourist information, planning data.

You have control over the images presented and the size of area to be studied; think about how to ensure the children get a broad view of the area from various perspectives.

8 Plan and deliver INSET to colleagues who will be working with you

Prepare colleagues and helpers for the visit by identifying the challenges and benefits of the plan for both teachers and the children, looking at how the activities develop geography and other subject areas.

Figure 22: A step-by-step approach to planning. A blank version of this planner is on page 62

PLACES

Features and character of places

By the end of Year 2
Describe the main features of localities they have studied, using appropriate geographical terms *(e.g. hill, river, factory)* and demonstrate *(e.g. orally, in pictures, in writing)* that they recognise those features that give localities their character *(e.g. busy shopping street, large flat fields).*

By the end of Year 4
Describe a range of physical and human features of localities studied, using appropriate geographical terms *(e.g. transport, industry, tributary)* and begin to offer reasons for the distinctive character of different places *(e.g. the coastal location and attractive scenery of a seaside resort).*

By the end of Year 6
Describe the physical and human features of a range of places studied and show how the mix of these features helps to explain their character *(e.g. explaining how the weather, landscape and human activities in a hill farming area make it very different from an urban locality).*

Contrasts and relationships between places

By the end of Year 2
Begin to recognise contrasts in individual features of different localities *(e.g. characteristics of houses in photographs of a tropical locality and their own locality).*

By the end of Year 4
Make geographical comparisons between the localities studied and begin to offer reasons for their findings, including reference to location *(e.g. referring to situation and weather when comparing the scenery and activities of a tropical locality with the home locality).*

By the end of Year 6
Draw out similarities and differences between places, including awareness of their wider geographical location *(e.g. which region; which country; which continent?)* and understanding of links between them *(e.g. trade between countries).*

PATTERNS AND PROCESSES

Patterns

By the end of year 2
Respond to questions about 'where things are', by making simple observations about features in the environment *(e.g. the shop is in the village centre, the pedestrian crossing is next to the school, summer is warmer than spring).*

By the end of year 4
Offer appropriate observations about locations and the patterns made by individual physical and human features in the environment *(e.g. hotels along the sea-front, frost on the northern side of the school playground).*

By the end of Year 6
Begin to appreciate the importance of location in understanding places and offer explanations for patterns of physical or human features *(e.g. explain why a town grew up at a river crossing).*

Physical and human processes

By the end of Year 2
Respond to questions about 'why things are like that', by recognising and making appropriate observations about physical features *(e.g. the heavy rain has flooded the school field)* and human features *(e.g. the village shop has closed because not enough people use it).*

By the end of year 4
Begin to explain 'why things are like that', referring to physical and human features of the landscape *(e.g. why factories near motorways can receive goods and materials easily, how exposure to sun or shade can affect snow conditions in ski resorts).*

By the end of year 6
Recognise selected physical and human processes *(e.g. river erosion, closure of a coal mine)* and begin to appreciate how these can change the character of places and environments they have studied.

Figure 23: The main features of progression and expectation in four aspects of learning geography

ENVIRONMENTAL RELATIONSHIPS AND ISSUES

Viewpoints and perspectives about the environment

By the end of year 2
Express their own views about the physical and/or human features of the environment in a locality *(e.g. a wild rocky landscape, a noisy street)*.

By the end of year 4
Begin to account for their own views about the environment, recognising that other people may have reasons for thinking differently *(e.g. explaining why a rocky coastline is attractive to them, but may be dangerous for fishermen)*.

By the end of year 6
Identify and explain the different views held by people about an environmental change *(e.g. the different views held by residents and the developer about plans to build a fast food restaurant)*.

Environmental interactions and management

By the end of year 2
Recognise how an environment changes and how people are affecting an environment, when asked 'what is this place like?' *(e.g. seasonal change in the landscape, rubbish tipped in a local beauty spot)*.

By the end of year 4
Identify how people affect the environment and recognise ways in which people try to manage it for the better *(e.g. recognise that restricting car access is one way to reduce air pollution in the local town)*.

By the end of year 6
Recognise and describe how people can improve or damage the environment in particular cases, and describe different approaches taken to management *(e.g. investigate alternative strategies for minimising erosion of a footpath)*.

GEOGRAPHICAL ENQUIRY AND SKILLS

Geographical enquiry

By the end of year 2
Ask and respond to questions about places and topics studied, on the basis of information provided by the teacher and their own observations *(e.g. recognise the main landscape features on a photograph)*.

By the end of year 4
Ask and respond to geographical questions *(e.g. why are there fewer trees on the hill top?)* in the course of undertaking tasks set by the teacher, and offer their own ideas appropriate to the situation *(e.g. suggestions for carrying out a fieldwork task)*.

By the end of year 6
Draw on their own observations and on secondary sources provided, and use their awareness of topical matters to suggest geographical questions and issues which might be studied *(e.g. impact of a hurricane, effect of a new local superstore)*.

Use of skills

By the end of year 2
Undertake simple tasks, using maps, diagrams and other secondary sources as demonstrated by the teacher *(e.g. use letter and number co-ordinates to identify a feature, draw a pictorial diagram of a shop in the High Street)*.

By the end of year 4
Use a range of simple pieces of equipment and secondary sources *(e.g. atlas, photographs, anemometer)* to carry out tasks supported by the teacher *(e.g. find the correct page in the atlas, measure the wind speed)*.

By the end of year 6
Use confidently a full range of skills (specified for key stage 2) and different kinds of maps and resources, to undertake some independent investigations and some planned by the teacher *(e.g. take measurements of river speed on fieldwork, record the results using IT, and plot them on a diagram)*.

Figure 23 cont'd: from 'Expectations in Geography at Key Stages 1 and 2' SCAA 1997

9: Planning and delivering INSET

The best approach is probably to introduce some practical activities before you delve into the Programmes of Study. INSET time could be used for a number of purposes. You could use it to decide on a locality to visit, or to consider a whole key stage plan. You could use the ideas on the following pages to devise practical experiences based on the activities described in this book (see preparation guidelines, pages 50-53). Consider the time you have available for INSET, the needs of the stage, the point you have reached in your curriculum planning for locality studies and then plan accordingly. Figures 24 and 25 suggests programmes for INSET periods of different durations; Figure 26 an INSET day involving a UK locality.

Activity	Purpose	Resources
1 Brainstorm to identify the benefits children gain from working outside on field visits. (15 mins)	Lays down a basic justification for the work as part of the curriculum.	Flip charts for group feedback.
2 Identify the features of the school's local area and then the features which would provide a contrast. (15 mins)	Develops a rationale for selecting contrasting localities over KS1 and 2.	Key words from geography PoS.
3 List resources which are needed to study a contrasting locality. Identify safety hazards to be aware of. (30 mins)	Determines feasibility of localities - are resources available and affordable?	Planning a safe locality study sheet.
4 Use some photographs to ask and answer the sort of geographical questions which children would use on a locality study. (30 mins)	Demonstrates how geographical skills and vocabulary can be developed.	Range of mounted photographs.
5 If there is time try out some practical activities in the playground or vicinity of school. (30mins)	Demonstrates ideas and techniques.	
6 Refer to the geography PoS and match statements with activities that you have tried. (30 mins)	Identifies how activities address elements of the PoS in geography and other subjects.	

Figure 24: A programme for a post-school (twilight) INSET session

Activity	Purpose
1 Activities 1 - 5 from the twilight session plus ...	As Figure 24
2 Try out some of the planned activities.	Allows teachers to adapt the activities, match them to ability levels, and consider associated practicalities
3 Plan the study of contrasting UK and distant localities over the whole key stage(s). Incorporate opportunities for a locality to be visited by successive year groups.	Ensure coherence for children's learning and builds in opportunities for progression.

Figure 25: A programme for a half or full day INSET session

Objectives

You are going to investigate the possibilities for developing geography through a place study. You will be focusing on several elements of the National Curriculum - you should be able to identify how each activity addresses a part of KS1 or 2.

Aims for locality work

To enable children to:

- investigate the physical and human features of their surroundings;
- ask geographical questions based on direct experience and fieldwork;
- recognise and explain geographical patterns;
- become aware of how places fit into a broader geographical context;
- observe, question and record, and to communicate ideas and information.

Programme

During the course of the day you have approximately three hours to complete a range of tasks, some of which address broader cross-curricular issues.

For each task you are asked to work through the following stages:

- Try out the activity yourself.
- Identify the benefits and challenges associated with each activity for you as a teacher and for the children as learners.
- Identify the areas of the geography PoS which are addressed through the activity. (Consider the opportunities for cross-curricular work).
- Note down the in-class preparation and follow-up that would be required.
- Consider organisational aspects - including safety issues - and keep a note of important points.
- Make notes about how you might adapt the activity to suit younger, older, more able, less able children, i.e. introduce differentiation.

Some of the activities you are asked to complete are at a more complex level, and would be suitable for junior classes, but all can be adapted to suit younger groups. The language used is vital - when you design an activity for your class you can judge how many 'geographical terms' they will be able to cope with. The activities you devise will need to take into account varying abilities present in your class. The INSET activities can be adapted for use during key stages 1 and 2 by changing the size (and proximity to school) of the area to be studied and the complexity of the children's activities. The ideas also provide guidance in setting up studies of the local area. You can use places close to the school to practice skills and techniques which can then be used in a less familiar contrasting locality. Display the results of your activities and discuss further adaptations and improvements to suit different age groups, needs and localities.

Figure 26: An example of an INSET day on discovering a UK locality

10: Preparation guidelines for the geographical activities

Putting the locality into context (Figure 11, see page 31)

The kind of questions for which answers are needed

- What do you already know about the locality, from first-hand knowledge or from other sources?
- Where are the locality boundaries in relation to the school?
- Where is the locality on an atlas map, on a small scale map, on a large scale map and on the NC maps?
- Find out what county the locality is part of, and the neighbouring counties.
- Find out what links the locality has with other places, for example, is it on a main road or rail route?
- What resources or sources of information would you use to introduce this locality to children?

The following activities need locality base maps with or without a grid as appropriate.

Land use mapping activities (Figure 12, see page 32)

Out in the locality

- Use one of the base maps of the locality and do a survey of land-use for the area allotted. Working in pairs generates the best ideas for follow-up work in school.
- Identify safety issues for children completing this activity and mark suitable places for group work on the map.

On return

- Devise a key to include all land use types in the area and complete a simple version of the base map appropriate for the key stage. You might need to show if buildings are used for more than one purpose, e.g. different usage on different floors, and then decide whether to record this with the older children (see Figure 27).
- What cross-curricular links do these activities develop?

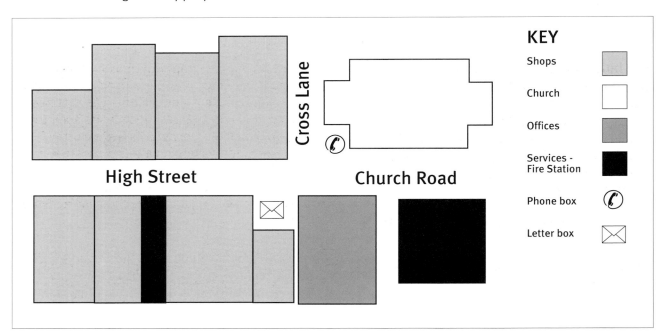

Figure 27: Land use near St James' Church

Observation trails (Figures 13, 14, 15 and 16, see pages 34, 35 and 36)

Out in the locality

- Walk around the area (shown on a base map with a grid) and familiarise yourself with the place.
- Take a series of photographs around the chosen area (or simply decide and list what you would photograph).
- Make notes for questions or activities to be used with each of the photos (see table below).

On return

- Devise an 'Observation Trail' to investigate the locality. Develop clues to encourage observation of the detail and the functions to be seen in the area.
- Decide the final form depending upon your curriculum needs. The trail could be used for a treasure hunt, a guide for children from a link school or a storyboard for a TV programme about the locality.
- Urban trails should encourage children to observe, draw, touch, explore, investigate. Consider using the **Sensory Walk** worksheet and **Cards** to encourage close observation.
- Try out the **Rainbow/Alphabet I-Spy**, **Different People** and **Let's Go Shopping**.

Map ref.	Photograph	Clue	Questions	Activity	PoS

The built environment (Figures 15, 16 and 18, see pages 36 and 38)

Out in the locality

- Use the **My Favourite Features** (Figure 16) and **Looking at Building Materials** (Figure 13) and **Word Pairs** (Figure 18) worksheets to investigate different aspects of the built environment. How could you follow this up, back in the classroom?
- There are some further ideas in the table for developing geographical thinking (page 18). See how many 'new' un-noticed features you can find. Make a video. Find areas that need attention and a street which lends itself to model making. Decide which are worthy features for putting on a tourist poster or leaflet.
- Enter your findings on a base map.
- What cross-curricular links do these activities develop?

Map ref.	Feature	Vocabulary	Preparation	Follow-up	PoS

The physical environment (Figure 17, see page 37)

Out in the locality

- Discover suitable locations in the playground, park or locality for items such as benches, and flower tubs which require sheltered conditions.
- Using the base map (north should be at the top of the map or shown with an arrow) mark contrasting locations, sunny spots, windy corners, damp dark places and so on, for children to carry out measuring activities in different weather conditions to learn about 'micro climates'.
- Make a decision about the possible best place.

On return

- Consider how to set up a preparatory discussion with a class.
- Do an audit of measuring equipment - are there enough wind meters? thermometers? rain gauges? What can be made in D & T and Science? What needs to be bought?
- What cross-curricular links do these activities develop?

Environmental quality investigations (Figure 18, page 38)

- Design some simple tests or techniques to collect data on pollution in the locality.
- How would you display your results on a map? Try it out.
- What cross-curricular links do these activities develop?

Question	Experiment	Mapping	Preparation	Follow-up	PoS

Surveys and data handling (Figure 19, page 39)

- Identify an issue which you could investigate using a simple survey (i.e. collecting, counting and using data).
- Design a survey sheet, questionnaire or tally sheet.
- Carry out your survey until you feel you have collected sufficient data to draw some broad conclusions. How will you judge this?
- Illustrate your results on a base map. Think about different methods of showing results on a map.
- What follow-up investigation activity could make use of the data collected?
- What cross-curricular links do these activities develop?

Issue	Type of Survey	Location	Time of Survey	Follow-up including IT	PoS

Changing building functions (Figure 20, page 41)

- Find a 'space' or building in your locality which is either:
  1 derelict
  2 has potential for development
  3 has changed function
  4 has become run down and uncared for.
- Mark it on a base map.
- Can you find out what it was like before? What sources will you use to find out about the site?

Site	Current use	Library	Maps	Photos	Local persons	PoS

Either Make a map of the site, showing how you would develop it, giving reasons why.

Or Draw a sketch of the site, showing how you would redevelop the space, and why.

Or Draw a field sketch of the building and its environs, annotating features (old and new) which give clues about (a) previous use and function; (b) current function; (c) major changes to structure or environment.

- Use an outline sheet such as Changing Functions (Figure 20) to record your work.
- Can you say why you think the changes have occurred? How would children form ideas about this? How would you prepare children for this type of work?
- You should think about which groups of people might be in favour or opposed to your proposals and how you would support or promote your case. How would you develop role-play based on this work?
- What cross-curricular links do these activities develop?
- This activity can take several teaching sessions (not all necessarily in Geography time). Use a proforma similar to the one below to develop a mini-scheme. This helps with planning both progression and differentiation.

Date	Concepts	Skills	Activity	Resources	Display	Assessment

An A4 photocopiable planning sheet for a six week enquiry investigation is in Figure 31 (page 61).

Planning a safe locality study

1 Before you decide on a locality ...
- Check your school/LEA policy regarding field visits.
- Check the insurance requirements for taking children out of the classroom.
- Establish the level of staffing and numbers of adult helpers (parents, trainee teachers etc.) available for the visit.
- Consider the age and ability of the children and the sort of locality they will be able to enjoy studying.
- Check that the coaches you will be using are fitted with safety equipment.

2 On a preliminary visit to the site ...
- Check booking procedures for any sites which require prior notification.
- Check on places which require permission to gain access.
- Identify potential hazards - water, roads, buildings, natural landscapes, building sites, other people.
- Determine whether hazards make the locality unsafe to visit.
- Take note of problems relating to extreme weather conditions - how will children be protected from wind, rain, sun etc.?
- Identify shelter and places to rest and eat lunches.
- Identify a safe place to disembark from the coach and gather as a large group. Find a safe meeting point.
- Establish what activities the children will be able to manage safely, including moving around the place.
- Find out where payphones and police stations are.

3 Before the children's visit ...
- Plan groups of children and allocate teachers and adults to work with them.
- Do the adults know the names of the children?
- Are the groups small enough for suitable and sufficient supervision?
- Establish clear safety procedures with adults and children.
- Identify emergency contacts.
- Brief adults about the activities, safety procedures and responses to problems. Make sure you have a first aid kit.
- Involve children in the safety planning - using the Road Safety code, the Countryside Code - and identifying potential hazards on maps.
- Explain what you want the children to do on the day in terms of geographical work and how to behave.

4 During the locality study ...
- Make sure everyone knows the time and place to be at meeting points.
- Make sure you know what everyone is doing at all times.
- Stick to the plan you have agreed - don't take chances or make compromises. It is better to cancel rather than take a risk!

Useful resources and addresses

Publications

Teachers' books

From the Geographical Association, 160 Solly Street, Sheffield S1 4BF:

Bowles, R. (1993) *Resources for Key Stages 1, 2 and 3*

Chambers, B. (1995) *Awareness into Action: Environmental Education in the Primary Curriculum.*

Milner, A. (1994) *Geography Starts Here!*

Milner, A. (1997) *Geography Through Play.*

Morgan, W. (1995) *Plans for primary geography.*

Norris Nicholson, H. (revised edition, 1996) *Place in Story Time.*

Smeaton, M. (ed) (1991) *Local Studies 5-13: KS1 & 2 Support Material.*

Primary Geographer (quarterly) contains valuable guidance on both teaching and ways of learning.

Environmental education

Copeland, T. (1992) *Geography and the Historic Environment.* English Heritage.

DES (1990) *Environmental Education 5-16.* HMSO.

Joicey, H. (1986) *An Eye on the Environment.* Bell & Hyman.

Mays, P. (1985) *Teaching Children Through the Environment.* Hodder & Stoughton.

Pluckrose, H. (1989) *Seen Locally.* Routledge.

Ross, A. (1990) *Bright Ideas: Geography in the Environment.* Scholastic.

Wilson, R. (1988) *Starting From a Walk.* Trentham Books.

Fieldwork

May, S. et al. (1993 onwards) *Fieldwork in Action* series. Geographical Association.

Wass, S. (1990) *Explorations: a Guide to Fieldwork in the Primary School.* Hodder & Stoughton.

The school grounds

Purkis, S. (1993) *A Teacher's Guide to Using School Buildings.*

English Heritage.

Young, K. and Lucas, B. (1990) *Using the School Grounds as a Resource.* Learning Through Landscapes Trust.

Further reading

Planning suggestions, resource and address lists are given in curriculum context in:

Bowles, R. (1992) *Practical Guides: Geography.* Scholastic.

Blyth, A. and Krause, J. (1995) *Primary Geography - a developmental approach.* Hodder & Stoughton.

Foley, M. and Janikoun, J. (1996) *The Really Practical Guide to Primary Geography,* (second edition). Stanley Thornes.

Hughes, J. and Marsden, W.E. (1994) *Primary School Geography.* David Fulton.

Palmer, J. (1994) *Geography in the Early Years.* Routledge.

Wiegand, P. (1992) *Places in the Primary School.* Falmer Press.

Wiegand, P. (1993) *Children and Primary Geography.* Cassell.

Articles in *Junior Education, Junior Focus, Child Education* and *Infant Projects* (monthly and bi-monthly from Scholastic) take up the themes followed by the above authors.

Locality resource kits

These can include aerial and ground photographs (P), data (D), maps (M) and suggestions for activities both inside and out of the classroom (A). They are not intended to replace a teacher visit but some include a video (V) which enables detailed work for a contrasting study. Chiefly aimed at key stage 2, but can all be adapted for key stage 1.

BBC Publications (1996) *Contrasting UK locality resource pack and video*: four BBC Zig-Zag programmes (7-9 yrs) on a comparison of Stanton in the Peak (Village) and nearby central Manchester (Urban). Highlights themes and geographical principles in an enquiry approach. Useful stimulant. BBC Publications. (P, D, M, A, V)

BBC Publications *Homes across Europe Resource Pack*: contrasting localities in Britain (London and Stockbridge), Greece and Finland for 5-7year olds (see below). BBC Publications. (P, A)

Bowles, R. (1994) *Geography Study Kits: 1) Plymouth - A Waterfront City; 2) Eyam - An English Village; 3) A Market Town - Bury St Edmunds.* Each has a full colour children's adventure story book in diary form using places illustrated in the locality pack. Scholastic. (P, D, M, A)

Bowles, R. and Harrison, S. (1997) *An Urban Locality: Clerkenwell, Central London.* Folens. (P, D, M, A)

Channel 4 Schools (1996) *The Local Network.* Complements Channel 4 Geography Junction. Visits 3 places - Colton village, Staffs.; the Old Dean Estate, Camberley, Surrey; Swansea City Centre. Suitable support for thematic work rather than in-depth locality work. Channel 4 Schools. (P, M, A, V)

Educational Television Company (1995) *Malham Tarn Resource Pack and Video*; Yorkshire Dales National Park/Educational Television Company. (P, M, A, V)

Harrison, P. and Harrison, S. (1995) *A Rural Locality: Sedbergh, Yorkshire Dales.* Folens. (P, D, M, A)

Jackson, E. and Morgan, W. (1994) *Flatford: A Contrasting UK Locality.* Geographical Association. (P, D, M, A)

Marsden, W.E. and Marsden, V. (1996) *A Victorian Seaside Resort: Southport.* Chris Kington Publishing.

Walker, G. (1995) *Discover Godstone.* Wildgoose Publications. (P, D, M, A)

Walker, G. and Garman, D. (1996) *Discover Croydon.* Wildgoose Publications. (P, D, M, A)

Wilson, P. (1995) *Betws-y-Coed: A Contrasting Locality in Wales.* Field Studies Council. (P, D, A)

Television series

New programmes are usually repeated over the following two or three years.

BBC
Watch (5-7 years)

Where we Live: 4 contrasting places: the city of Edinburgh; a strawberry farm in Kent; Tenby, a Welsh seaside town; and the River Bann, Ireland. Available on video.

Geography: Our Environment: compares environments with own locality; develops vocabulary and skills in observation, recording and communication (Resource pack available).

Geography: Homes across Europe (see above)

Zig-Zag (7-9 years)

Village, Town and City (also Fact Finder book, resource pack and video) addresses the KS2 Settlement theme requirements.

Where I live, Where you Live (see *Contrasting UK pack* above) addresses the KS2 Place requirements.

Geography UK: (also Fact Finder, Resource Pack and video) addresses the KS2 themes including Environmental Change in a UK context.

Landmarks (9-12 years)

Local History Project the last programme (of 5) looks at the development of Basingstoke (Resource pack and video available).

Portrait of Britain: 5 case studies - The Isle of Skye; Stoke City; Peterborough New Town; London a capital city; Folkestone/Dover - gateway to Europe (extends the work begun in the Zig-Zag UK programme and resources)

The River Severn: a journey from source to mouth addressing geographical themes and historical features. (Resource pack and video available)

Treasures of the Landscape: Journey on mountain bikes looking at the foundations of landscapes using geological and physical geography clues with map reading.

Channel 4
Stop, Look, Listen (5-7 years)

Streetwise, Places and Journeys, People Who Help Us: all three units develop geographical skills and concepts using information from the local environment and other places in the wider world (activity books and videos available).

Geography Junction (7-11 years)

These programmes provide material i) for developing expertise in understanding similarities and differences, ii) recognising environmental issues. Each programme has teacher guides; some are available as videos.

Whose Place?: Snowdonia, motorways, Nottingham, St Lucia, the Rhine.

Over the Border: Geographical characteristics of urban and rural Scotland.

Bus Stop: An enquiry approach to comparing the home locality with Welsh localities including the Rhondda, Snowdonia, Wrexham, and Cardiff.

Down to Earth: Thematic studies based upon Northern Ireland environments.

Computer software
Floppy disks

Weather Watch (1992) N. Willink/SoftTeach
Easily managed database and graphic files plus extra files for comparison of own records with another locality. You can create your own library to compare year by year and with link schools. Clear guide, worksheets. All platforms available on approval.

Local Studies (1995) Bartholomew Ramsey/ SoftTeach
Simple map making program which can also use OS digital map data from your local authority. Simple base maps can be created with pictogram or conventional symbols to suit your own locality studies. Clear guide, worksheets, ready made files for practising mapping skills in specific places (Shops, Street, Farm, Market). All platforms available on approval.

CD-ROM

Ordnance Survey Interactive Atlas of Great Britain (1996) OS/Attica, Milton Keynes.
This allows you to set localities in context and plan routes between places. There are map skill exercises to support the work, plus glossary and gazetteer.

Land use (1997) Staffordshire Schools and Advisers/Matrix Multimedia Ltd.
Aerial photographs, Land Use-UK and OS maps for over 45 selected 1km squares at 1:10 000 scale. Simple description of enquiry approach and activity sheets, including writing frames, can be tailored to different top junior abilities. Useful to develop comparisons and similar enquiries with home area.

Discover York (1995) OS/NRSC/Wildgoose Publications.
Continuous aerial cover, OS map cover at several scales plus hot spots for detailed ground information. Good preparation for a visit and follow up.

Discover London (1997) OS/NRSC/Wildgoose Publications.
Similar to *Discover York* for specific localities but more tourist information.

County/Locality Series: Northamptonshire, Manchester and Merseyside
Resource discs of 100 aerial views with facilities to draw maps and diagrams based upon the views for presentation.

Sources of information

Large-scale maps and plans
Goad mapping
Experian Goad Ltd
Goad House
Salisbury Square
Hatfield
Hertfordshire AL9 5BJ
01707 271171

Education Team
Ordnance Survey
Romsey Road
Southampton SO16 4GU
01703 792960
(or contact your local Approved Ordnance Survey Educational Supplier. Also a source of old maps of a locality)

The National Map Centre●
22-24 Caxton Street
London SW1H 0QU
0171 222 2466

Latitude● (personal shopping and
mail order)
34 The Broadway
Darkes Lane
Potters Bar
Herts EN6 2HW
(also Goad shopping plans and
aerial photographs)
01707 663090

● Educational Discount. Both
approved National OS Agents

Aerial photographs and satellite images
Earth Images
P O Box 43
Keynsham
Bristol BS18 2TH
0117 986 1144

PhotoAir
191a Main Street
Yaxley
Peterborough PE7 3LD
01733 241850

The Meteorological Office
Education Services
Johnson House
London Road
Bracknell RG12 2SY
01344 854818

Wildgoose Publications
The Reading Room
Dennis Street
Hugglescote
Leicestershire LE67 2FP
01530 835685
Supplies all educational products
previously obtained from the
National Remote Sensing Centre
(NRSC), including aerial photo
packs and resource packs plus CD-
ROMS (see above).

Hunting Aerofilms
Gate Studios
Station Road
Boreham Wood
Herts WD6 1EJ
0181 207 0666

Heritage and local history
English Heritage
Education Service
429 Oxford Street
London W1R 2HD
0171 973 3442

Environmental organisations with an interest in UK locality issues
Friends of the Earth
Freepost
56-58 Alnia Street
Luton LU1 2YZ
01582 482297

Common Ground
Seven Dials Warehouse
44 Earlham Street
London WC2H 9LA
0171 379 3109
An environmental charity that
offers ideas and information to
help people learn about their
locality.

Council for Environmental
Education
0118 975 6061 (Information
Service)
An umbrella group providing
information for schools and links
with environmental organisations.

The Pedestrian Association
126 Aldersgate Street
London EC1A 4JQ
0171 608 0353

Sustrans (schools)
35 King Street
Bristol BS1 4DZ
0117 929 0888
Safe Routes to School Project.

Waste Watch
24 Holborn Viaduct
London EC1A 2BN
0171 248 1818
Organises community recycling
schemes.

Television programmes and support materials
Channel 4
Schools
P O Box 100
Warwick CV34 6TZ
01926 433333

BBC Education
White City
London W12 7TS
0181 746 1111

Field studies
Field Studies Council
Preston Montford
Montford Bridge
Shrewsbury SY4 1HW
01743 850674

The Council for Environmental
Education
School of Education
University of Reading
London Road
Reading RG1 5AQ
0118 975 6061

School links and twinning
International Committee
The Geographical Association
160 Solly Street
Sheffield
S1 4BF
0114 296 0088

Publishers of locality studies
Scholastic Educational Books
FREEPOST CV 3067
Leamington Spa
Warwickshire CV33 0BR
01926 816216

Folens Publishers
Albert House
Apex Business Centre
Boscombe Road
Dunstable LU5 4RL
01582 472788

Chris Kington Publishing
27 Rathmore Road
Cambridge CB1 4AB
01223 240030

Software publishers
SoftTeach
Sturgess Farmhouse
Longbridge Deverill
Warminster
Wilts BA12 7EA
01985 840329

Attica
Media House
Presley Way
Crownhill
Milton Keynes MK8 0ES
01908 570113

Matrix Multimedia Ltd
10 Hey Street
Bradford BD7 1DQ
01274 730808

Photocopiable forms and grids

GEOGRAPHICAL ENQUIRY PLANNING SHEET   Focus for enquiry   Year:

Enquiry stage	Activities	PoS	Classroom preparation	Differentiation	Resources	Assessment from NC Level Descriptions
Identify key questions you would ask children to investigate.						
Identify what data needs to be collected and how it will be gathered.						
Identify the ways in which the data will be interpreted.						
Identify how conclusions might be arrived at.						

Figure 28: Geographical enquiry planning sheet

A	B	C	D

Figure 29: Photocopiable large scale grid overlay. Enlarge, copy onto acetate and use as overlays on base maps and other maps

page **59**

10

9

8

7

6

5

4

3

2

1

Figure 30: Photocopiable small scale grid overlay. Enlarge, copy onto acetate and use as overlays on base maps and other maps

Term   Class   Subject   Teacher

Date/Week	Questions	PoS	Knowledge/ Skills	Activities/ Visits	Resources	Language Opportunities	Numeracy Opportunities	Display/ Outcomes/ Assessment

Figure 31: Photocopiable six-week planner sheet

| **1 Curriculum aims:** | KS | KS links | |
| | Year | Class | Term |

2 Possible place/locality		
Size	Location	Theme
Skills	Literacy	Numeracy
IT	Cross-curricular	

3 Visits/Resource collection and provision

4 Enquiry focus:

Major activities

5 Programme of Study elements:

| KS1 | 1a,b,c | 2 | 3a,b,c,d,e,f | 4 | 5a,b,c,d | 6 | | | | |
| KS2 | 1a,b,c | 2a,b,c | 3a,b,c,d,e,f | 4 | 5a,b,c,d,e | 6 | 7a,b | 8a,b,c | 9a,b,c | 10a,b |

6 Activities: Preparation
Needs
Display

7 Resources

8 INSET

Figure 32: A proforma for planning contrasting and distant place activities